NAVAL POSTGRADUATE SCHOOL

MONTEREY, CALIFORNIA

THESIS

INVISIBLE SOLDIERS: INTEGRATION AND MOTIVATIONS OF WOMEN WITHIN BOKO HARAM AND THE CROSS-REGIONAL TRENDS OF FEMALE TERRORISM

by

Sarah E. Erickson

June 2019

Thesis Advisor:	Jessica R. Piombo
Second Reader:	Carolyn C. Halladay

Approved for public release. Distribution is unlimited.

THIS PAGE INTENTIONALLY LEFT BLANK

INVISIBLE SOLDIERS: INTEGRATION AND MOTIVATIONS OF WOMEN WITHIN BOKO HARAM AND THE CROSS-REGIONAL TRENDS OF FEMALE TERRORISM

Sarah E. Erickson
Lieutenant, United States Navy
BA, University of Rochester, 2014

Submitted in partial fulfillment of the
requirements for the degree of

MASTER OF ARTS IN SECURITY STUDIES
(MIDDLE EAST, SOUTH ASIA, SUB-SAHARAN AFRICA)

from the

NAVAL POSTGRADUATE SCHOOL
June 2019

Approved by: Jessica R. Piombo
                Advisor

                Carolyn C. Halladay
                Second Reader

                Afshon P. Ostovar
                Associate Chair for Research
                Department of National Security Affairs

iii

iv

ABSTRACT

Over the past century, women have been increasingly integrated and utilized within terrorist organizations. This thesis analyzes Boko Haram as a case study and examines the unique roles that women hold within it, focusing on the voluntary and involuntary motivations women participants use to justify their activity within the extremist organization. It examines the new ways in which female insurgents are being integrated into the organization and how this increased involvement, particularly as suicide bombers, lends to the effectiveness of Boko Haram as a terrorist organization. To conclude, this thesis discusses the measures that both the Nigerian and U.S. governments must take in order to help effectively combat Boko Haram. The measures taken must integrate women into the foundation of restructured government institutions in order for equality and education across religious and gender lines to be reached. Through this process, the root grievances of the Nigerian people and Boko Haram insurgency are addressed and eradication of the organization is made possible.

THIS PAGE INTENTIONALLY LEFT BLANK

TABLE OF CONTENTS

LIST OF ACRONYMS AND ABBREVIATIONS

ANPP   All Nigeria People's Party

CJTF   Civilian Joint Task Force

CNA   Center for Naval Analysis

COIN   Counterinsurgency

FTO   Foreign Terrorist Organization

IDP   Internally Displaced Person

IEA   Islamic Emirate of Afghanistan

ISI   Pakistani Secret Service

JRA   Japanese Red Army

LGA   Local Government Area

LTTE   Liberation Tigers of Tamil Eelam

PKK   Partiya Karkerên Kurdistan

PSYOP   Psychological Operations

RIRA   Real Irish Republican Army

RPG   Rocket Propelled Grenade

THIS PAGE INTENTIONALLY LEFT BLANK

ACKNOWLEDGMENTS

I would like to thank my husband for his unyielding support in all of my endeavors. Your faith in me led me to return to pursue this degree and has carried me through when I was not sure I would make it. Your faith and support were invaluable to me throughout this process. I cannot wait to have free weekends to go camping and on adventures with you and the dogs.

I would like to thank my parents and sisters—Mike, Cheryl, Megan, and Hannah—who have never stopped believing in me. Thank you for teaching me the value of hard work and education while never letting me give up on my goals. Thank you for instilling my sense of adventure and love of learning about the world and different cultures. Now that this thesis is over, my bucket list can begin!

Last, I would like to thank Dr. Jessica Piombo and Dr. Carolyn Halladay for their time and patience throughout this thesis process and my time at the Naval Postgraduate School. Your advice, insight, and editing were invaluable and I truly appreciate everything that you did for me.

THIS PAGE INTENTIONALLY LEFT BLANK

I.   INTRODUCTION

> To assume that violence is not a feminine characteristic and that women are not capable of mass murder has obvious appeal: it allows for hope that at least half the human race will not devour the other, that it will protect children and so safeguard the future.

> —Wendy Lower[1]

When the discussion of terrorism comes up, most people do not immediately visualize a woman as the perpetrator. This presumption may owe to a preconceived feminine identity, that characterizes women as mothers, sisters, wives, friends—and inherently non-violent and passive. Yet over the past century, women have been increasingly integrated and utilized within terrorist organizations.[2] Since the early 1960s, this increased female involvement in terrorist organizations has sparked an increase in academic interest in the motivations, integration, and psychology behind women's roles in these organizations. In turn, new insights are emerging; for example, women are not simply being coerced into participation, but they are voluntarily seeking out more and more violent roles.[3] For another example, since the first reported case of a Boko Haram female suicide bomber on June 8, 2014, the rate of female suicide bombers has steadily increased, and women have now become the preferred gender for suicide bombings carried out by this terrorist organization.[4]

With the evolution of modern conflict, women have been increasingly integrated into all aspects of terrorism. This thesis analyzes Boko Haram as a case study of the unique roles that women hold within it, focusing on the voluntary and involuntary

---

[1] Wendy Lower, *Hitler's Furies: German Women in the Nazi Killing Fields*, Reprint (Wilmington, MA: Mariner Books, 2014), 158.

[2] Katherine Lindemann, "Female Terrorists - A Surprisingly Timeless Phenomenon," *Researchgate* (blog), December 21, 2015, https://www.researchgate.net/blog/post/female-terrorists-a-surprisingly-timeless-phenomenon.

[3] Mia Bloom, *Bombshell: Women and Terrorism* (Philadelphia, PA: University of Pennsylvania Press, 2011), 233.

[4] Ania Skinner, "The Rising Trend of Female Suicide Bombers in Nigeria," *The Fund for Peace - Global Square* (blog), March 28, 2015, http://library.fundforpeace.org/blog-20150328-nigeriawomenbombers.

motivations women participants use to justify their activity within the extremist organization.[5] It examines the new ways in which female insurgents are being integrated into the organization, and how this increased involvement, particularly as suicide bombers, lends to the effectiveness of Boko Haram as a terrorist organization. Through this analysis, it can be understood how Boko Haram's tactics and utilization of women differs from its cross-regional counterparts and how this organization must be approached by the international community differently than its extremist counterparts in order to fully combat and eradicate it from the Lake Chad region.

In addition, the thesis addresses the following questions: Are there unique recruitment tactics that Boko Haram—compared to other contemporary extremist organizations—is implementing to control its female martyrs? Are the themes and trends—such as the kidnapping and torture of Christian women—that are being observed within the Boko Haram organization congruent with or similar to cross-regional narratives of extremist organizations located in differing regions and cultures? Additionally, how might the international community use this information to combat Boko Haram more effectively?

A.   OVERVIEW OF BOKO HARAM

The terrorist organization, Jama'a Ahl as-Sunna Lida'wa wa-al Jihad, which is translated to "People Committed to the Propagation of the Prophet's Teachings and Jihad" and is more commonly referred to and recognized as Boko Haram, has actively opposed the influence of Western culture and education in northern Nigeria, Cameroon, Niger, and Mali.[6] In November 2013, the United States declared Boko Haram a Foreign Terrorist Organization (FTO).[7] As defined by the United States Immigration and

---

[5] The term "terrorist organization" and "extremist organization" will be used interchangeably throughout this literature.

[6] Patricio Asfura-Heim and Julia McQuaid, "Diagnosing the Boko Haram Conflict: Grievances, Motivations, and Institutional Resilience in Northeast Nigeria," *CNA Analysis & Solutions*, January 2015, xiii.

[7] "Foreign Terrorist Organizations," U.S. Department of State, accessed August 6, 2017, https://www.state.gov/j/ct/rls/other/des/123085.htm.

Nationality Act, FTOs are foreign organizations who engage in terrorist activity that actively endanger U.S. citizens or U.S. national security.[8]

Established in 2002 by Mohammed Yusuf, Boko Haram was a relatively peaceful movement comprised primarily of Kanuri people who aspired to bring Islamic ideologies and religiously based government institutions to the people of northern Nigeria, as they felt that their ethnic group was being economically repressed by the Nigerian government. After a violent altercation with police in 2009 in which Yusuf was killed, Boko Haram took a one-year hiatus to regroup and reemerge with the mission of revenge. Since then, Boko Haram has gained notoriety for its kidnapping of Christian women and children throughout northern Nigeria and its use of women in suicide operations.[9]

In order to understand how to combat this new wave of fighters within this organization, one must understand the motivations of these women as well as the different ways in which they have been integrated into the Boko Haram insurgency. This insight, in comparison with historical cases of female insurgents throughout three other FTOs located in different regions around the world, will provide a cross-regional analysis of four extremist Islamic organizations. All of these organizations vary considerably on the cultural scale due to their geographic location, or global presence, and consequently how they organize their FTOs in regards to the utilization of their women. Boko Haram, for example, has utilized women in a combative role since its resurgence in 2009, just as the Chechen Black Widows did, whereas Al-Qaeda and the Afghani Taliban were much slower to integrate women into both supporting and combative roles. These three cross-regional FTOs have been analyzed and provide valuable insight into an underrated but integral part of terrorist organizations, thus contributing to the larger road map of how to most effectively restore peace and stability to northern Nigeria, Cameroon, Niger, and Mali.

---

[8] Department of Homeland Security, "Immigration and Nationality Act: Section 219," 8 USC § 1189 (2001), https://www.uscis.gov/ilink/docView/SLB/HTML/SLB/0-0-0-1/0-0-0-29/0-0-0-5017.html#0-0-0-220.

[9] "Mapping Militant Organizations: Boko Haram," Stanford University, CISAC, August 26, 2016, 1–2, http://web.stanford.edu/group/mappingmilitants/cgi-bin/groups/view/553?highlight=boko+haram.

B. WOMEN IN TERRORISM: A LITERATURE REVIEW

Based on the stereotypical Western image of terrorists, it is a common misperception that women are not acting of their own accord when they participate in these extremist organizations. According to some, the concept of women as terrorists is disturbing, foreign and not a concept that generally fits the Western narrative and gender constructs that label women as nurturers and the passive, non-violent sex.[10] Mia Bloom explains that "many people have assumed that women could not consciously choose to participate in terrorism of their own volition. The underlying assumption is that a man made her do it."[11] This assumption though, contradicts the active participation and voluntary service that women have provided throughout history within terrorist organizations. The mobilization and value of women in both leadership and support positions have increased considerably along with the number of female suicide bombers in recent years. Thus, it is imperative that U.S. military leaders have a fuller understanding of the current and growing threat that these women pose to national security and international peace. This literature review explores why, in general, various terrorist organizations globally utilize women, how women become participants, as well as what roles women are filling and the contributions they are making to these FTOs.

> Although "terrorism" is one of the most widely used words in both international relations and the news media, the word lacks a clear, universal definition. Those who try to characterize it often harbor underlying biases (rendering their definitions questionable), or, in the case of some governments and the media, they may seek to label as many events as possible with a provocative term to demonize a particular group or to create headlines.[12]

Nonetheless, the term "terrorism" must be defined for the purpose of this thesis. Author Walter Laqueur observed that the earliest definition can be traced to the

---

[10] R. Kim Cragin and Sara A. Daly, *Women as Terrorists: Mothers, Recruiters, and Martyrs*, First (Santa Barbara, CA: ABC-CLIO, LLC, 2009), 1.

[11] Mia Bloom, *Bombshell: Women and Terrorism* (Philadelphia, PA: University of Pennsylvania Press, 2011), ix.

[12] Ellie B. Hearne, "Participants, Enablers, and Preventers: The Roles of Women in Terrorism," in *British International Studies Association Annual Conference* (Leicaster, UK, 2009), 2, https://is.muni.cz/el/1423/jaro2010/MVZ203/Gender___Terrorism__BISA__Hearne__Dec_2009.pdf.

Dictionnaire of the Académie Française, which defined the term terrorism as "système, régime de la terreur,"[13] thus claiming that even in its earliest form, the term "implied political upheaval, chaos, and violence."[14] This background leads to the modern understanding of the three recognized characteristics of terrorism—"violent tactics, nonstate actors, and political objectives."[15] For the purpose of this thesis, the definition given by Brian Michael Jenkins—that "terrorism may properly refer to a specific set of actions the primary intent of which is to produce fear and alarm that may serve a variety of purposes"—will be sufficient as it has built on the Académie Française definition and is constructed for modern terrorism.[16]

1. Why Use Women?

Terrorist organizations are rational actors that calculate the tactical purpose and strategic value of every action. The rise in the use of female operatives throughout extremist organizations can be seen as a shift in strategy both politically and tactically.[17] The traditional societal roles that women play—wife, mother, and nurturer—can be used both for and against extremist organizations. The path that women will take and the roles they come to play rely heavily on the women's circumstances upon first contact with the organization. Whether these women are widows, survivors of gender-based violence, or refugees has a large impact on how vulnerable they are to being coerced into subscribing to extremist ideology and enlisting in terrorist organizations.

The first major reason for the recruitment of women into extremist organizations is that women are much more capable of mobilizing support between both genders.[18] Women are generally able to attract more people to their organization than their male

---

[13] Cragin and Daly, *Women as Terrorists: Mothers, Recruiters, and Martyrs,* 7.

[14] Cragin and Daly, 7.

[15] Cragin and Daly, 7.

[16] Brian Michael Jenkins, "The Study of Terrorism: Definitional Problems" (Santa Monica, CA: RAND, December 1980), 2, http://www.dtic.mil/docs/citations/ADA103363.

[17] Katharina Von Knop, "The Female Jihad: Al Qaeda's Women," *Studies in Conflict & Terrorism* 30, no. 5 (2007): 400–401, https://doi.org/10.1080/10576100701258585.

[18] Von Knop, 401.

counterparts as they are seen as softer personalities, which allows them to appear more trustworthy when engaging with the population and recruiting new extremists. Women are also sought after to serve as incentive for male recruits, by fulfilling the sexual and domestic roles and duties of (ideologically committed) wives.[19]

Female terrorists are being idolized within their communities and seen as strong role models for other women, as well as shaming of men into enlistment.[20] Von Knop explains that "following the first female Palestinian suicide attack in January 2002, the Egyptian Islamist weekly newspaper *Al-Sha'ab* taunted, 'It is a woman, a woman, a woman who is a source of pride for the women of this nation and a source of honor that shames the submissive men with a shame that cannot be washed away except by blood.'"[21] By challenging men's masculinity, and giving them the chance to prove that they are "real men," extremist organizations are able to keep enlistment numbers rising. The enlistment of women and their use of shaming men into enlistment is a very popular tactic in ensuring the survival of the extremist organization when recruitment is low.[22]

Women also tend to attract widespread publicity, which then allows their organization to disseminate its message to a larger audience.[23] Bloom states that, "attacks are done for effect, and the more dramatic the effect, the stronger the message; thus a potential interest on the part of some groups in recruiting women."[24] By using women within their ranks, extremist organizations are able to gain media attention from around the world, which allows them to spread their message and stir up reactions from a larger audience. By gaining publicity, extremist organizations gain legitimacy, and by gaining legitimacy they are able to survive—even if their women members do not.

---

[19] International Crisis Group, *Nigeria: Women and the Boko Haram Insurgency* (Brussels, Belgium: International Crisis Group, 2016), 6, https://www.crisisgroup.org/africa/west-africa/nigeria/nigeria-women-and-boko-haram-insurgency.

[20] Von Knop, "The Female Jihad: Al Qaeda's Women," 401.

[21] Von Knop, 401.

[22] Von Knop, 401.

[23] Von Knop, 401.

[24] Bloom, *Bombshell: Women and Terrorism*, 22.

Indeed, women are being used for their effectiveness in carrying out missions. Bloom states that, "the underlying message conveyed by female bombers is: terrorism is no longer a fringe phenomenon and the insurgents are all around you."[25] Women are much more successful than men when it comes to kill rate and completion of bombing. "[Women are] the ultimate asymmetric weapon,"[26] says Magnus Ranstorp, the director of the Center for the Study of Terrorism and Political Violence. By using women in suicide campaigns, they can more easily avoid being caught by soldiers and security personnel as they do not fit the profiles and stereotypes of a terrorist that these forces are on the lookout for.[27] Many women in extremist organizations are able to conceal explosives around their mid-section in the disguise of a late-term pregnancy.[28] This tactic for concealing explosives allows them to bypass security personnel more effectively and blend in with the population, their target. Though accurate statistics are not available, as data collection on bombers and casualties is continually changing, the reasons behind using women as suicide bombers are known.

Finally, terrorist organizations use the capture and in some cases abuse of women to seek revenge and gain leverage over opponents, proving to the organization's opponents that they are unable to protect their women, thus also striking at their masculinity.[29] This tactic is particularly employed within the Boko Haram organization, which carried out its first kidnapping operation in February of 2013 with the sole purpose of retaliating against government officials.[30]

---

[25] Bloom, 24.

[26] Debra D. Zedalis, "Female Suicide Bombers" (U.S. Army War College: Strategic Studies Institute, 2004), 7, https://ssi.armywarcollege.edu/pdffiles/pub408.pdf.

[27] Bloom, *Bombshell: Women and Terrorism*, 20.

[28] Bloom, 21–22.

[29] Jacob Zenn and Elizabeth Pearson, "Women, Gender and the Evolving Tactics of Boko Haram," *Journal of Terrorism Research* 5, no. 1 (February 2014): 47–51, https://doi.org/10.15664.

[30] Zenn and Pearson, 47.

2. How Do Women Contribute?

The historical roles of women within extremist organizations are categorized into six functional roles by Kim Cragin and Sara Daly as: logisticians, recruiters, martyrs, operational leaders, guerrillas, and political vanguard.[31] These roles have been categorized by other academics as: preventers and enablers; supporters and perpetrators; and sympathizers, spies, warriors, and leaders.[32]

Cragin and Daly note that "logistics relate to the 'procurement, maintenance, and transportation of military material, facilities, and personnel; the handling of the details of an operation.' For terrorist or insurgent groups, logisticians smuggle weapons and funds to terrorist leaders and their operational cells."[33] As Cragin and Daly explain, women recruiters are "individuals used or designated by terrorist leaders to attract new logisticians, financiers, suicide bombers, or guerrilla fighters into their organization. Recruiters also often serve as essential linkages between a terrorist or insurgent group and popular support communities."[34] Though female political vanguards tend to be rare within terrorist organizations, they do exist. Cragin and Daly identify a few as "Kesire Yildirim from the Partiya Karkerên Kurdistan (PKK), … Bernadette Sands-McKevitt from the Real Irish Republican Army (RIRA) in Northern Ireland; Comandante Ramona from the Zapatista Revolutionary Army … in Mexico; … and even Fusako Sigenobu from the Japanese Red Army (JRA)."[35] Women tend to fall within three different categories of political vanguard: the strategic visionaries, who are women that revolutionize the ideology and strategy of a terrorist organization; the central committee members, who are women that participate in decision-making bodies within the organization; and finally the political officials, who have been elected to civilian

---

[31] Cragin and Daly, *Women as Terrorists: Mothers, Recruiters, and Martyrs*, 105.

[32] Hearne, "Participants, Enablers, and Preventers: The Roles of Women in Terrorism," 3.

[33] Cragin and Daly, *Women as Terrorists: Mothers, Recruiters, and Martyrs*, 21.

[34] Cragin and Daly, 39.

[35] Cragin and Daly, 87.

legislatures and are able to voice the opinions and needs of the terrorist organization to which they belong.[36]

Women have increasingly served in roles that directly put them within the line of fire or in positions where they are committing acts of violence against others. Boko Haram started to utilize women in suicide missions in 2011, with the younger women suspected of being forced into participation and the elder women of volunteering.[37] According to Von Knop, "suicide bombers provide a low-cost, low-technology, low-risk weapon that maximizes target destruction and instills fear—women are even more effective with their increased accessibility and media shock value."[38] Women hold incredible value to terrorist organizations as suicide bombers, which is why this trend is seemingly on the rise, not just in Boko Haram, but globally.

Regardless of motivations or integration though, it is evident that female involvement in terrorist organizations can no longer be put on the sideline when evaluating courses of action. Women are more essential to terrorist organizations than ever before. As Bloom conclusively states, "leaders of terrorist movements routinely make cost-benefit calculations to select the most effective tactics, targets, and operatives. Their analysis has shown that women are deadly."[39]

3. Pathways to Recruitment in Extremist Organizations

Women's roles in terrorism are increasingly diverse and complicated. Their experiences range from attempting to prevent violence and extremist organizations from growing and thriving to actively participating and facilitating this violence. Carol Cohn explains:

> Women are raped, tortured, maimed, and murdered, they are widowed, the children they have nurtured are lost to violence; but women are also members and supporters of the of the militaries and armed groups that commit these acts. Women stay home, resolutely striving to sustain family

---

[36] Cragin and Daly, 87–88.

[37] International Crisis Group, *Nigeria: Women and the Boko Haram Insurgency*, 10.

[38] Von Knop, "The Female Jihad: Al Qaeda's Women," 401.

[39] Bloom, *Bombshell: Women and Terrorism*, 34.

and community relationships; and women are displaced, living in camps without any of the structures that they have built to make life possible. Women are empowered by taking on new roles in wartime, and disempowered by being abducted from their homes and forced into armed groups or military prostitution.[40]

Women, both coerced and willing volunteers, have become increasingly involved in every aspect of terrorism, arguably more so than their male counterparts in that in many cultures, women both single and married will fill the supporting roles of mothers, teachers, and wives.[41] Their motivations can be encapsulated into five main categories: revenge, relationship, respect, redemption, and rape.[42] These motivations can be broken up into two main pathways to recruitment: voluntary and involuntary.

a. *Voluntary*

The voluntary motivations and subsequent enlistment of women, though not significantly different than their male counterparts, trend toward women with violent ideology being a product of their environment. This phenomenon can best be understood as "a radicalization process, rather than a one-time choice to join or not join a terrorist organization."[43] Radicalization into extremist organizations is the largest motivating factor as well as enlistment avenues for women who voluntarily join. As Cragin and Daly describe, the radicalization process has three components: availability, recruitment and indoctrination, and action.[44] Availability depends on an individual's circumstances prior to being exposed to the extremist organization, whether that is discrimination, oppression, pressures from family or friends, or conflict.[45] Recruitment and indoctrination takes place as soon as first contact is made between the organization and potential recruit. This first contact can be done through family members, friends, recruiters within the

---

[40] Carol Cohn, ed., *Women & Wars* (Cambridge, UK: Polity Press, 2013), 1–2.

[41] Bloom, *Bombshell: Women and Terrorism*, 30.

[42] Bloom, 235–36.

[43] Cragin and Daly, *Women as Terrorists: Mothers, Recruiters, and Martyrs*, 15.

[44] Cragin and Daly, 15–16.

[45] Cragin and Daly, 15.

community.[46] Individuals also can seek out and volunteer for terrorist organizations or they may have been tapped to perform a specific role or mission.[47] The last stage of radicalization is action. Cragin and Daly explain that women typically have the same indoctrination experiences and tests as men during this state of radicalization. This indoctrination process could be in the form of training camps or in smaller armed conflicts throughout the region. Participating in minor armed conflicts consequently allows women to prove that they have the same loyalty and commitment to their organization and cause as their male counterparts.[48]

Revenge has been cited as one of the largest influencers and motivators for female enlistment in extremist organizations, whether it is to avenge the death of a close family member or retaliate for past wrongs committed against the woman herself.[49] Relationship, as Bloom explains, is the best indicator of if and how involved a woman is likely to be engaged in violence.[50] While this method is not direct coercion, the pressure felt by women who either marry into the organization or have family members within the insurgency is generally enough to incorporate them into the system. In many cases, if a woman becomes a widow within the extremist organization, she will be immediately remarried to another member. This promise of security is enough for many women to seek relationships within extremist organizations. Respect also plays a large role in the decision of many women to join. Female suicide bombers are considered role models in their communities, as it shows that they have just as much commitment to the cause as their male counterparts, essentially making them posthumous celebrities.[51]

Redemption, the last voluntary trend, occurs when women are trying to make up for past sins or any scandalous acts that they have committed prior to first contact with the extremist organization. As Bloom indicates, "there have been reports that recruiters

---

[46] Cragin and Daly, 15.

[47] Cragin and Daly, 16.

[48] Cragin and Daly, 16.

[49] Bloom, *Bombshell: Women and Terrorism*, 235.

[50] Bloom, 235.

[51] Bloom, 236.

approach their targets by making romantic advances, literally seducing them into joining the group and then involving them in suicide operations."[52] Extremist organizations offer the hope of erasing all culturally embarrassing and scandalous transgressions of women's pasts through martyrdom. They offer them the chance to change their family reputation from shameful to heroic.[53]

b. *Involuntary*

Perhaps the most disturbing motivation and recruitment strategy though is rape, and the mental manipulation that rape has on women.[54] While not every woman in the world who is raped joins a terrorist organization, the women within conflict zones who are subjected to gender violence are particularly vulnerable to joining extremist organizations. They can be seeking revenge, redemption, and the promise of relationship by organization members if they have been ostracized from their home communities. Of note, this method of recruitment is not directly involuntary; these women still have the free will and ability to choose not to join. Still there is a close connection. For example, rape survivors in the Liberation Tigers of Tamil Eelam (LTTE) have been reported as joining in search of redemption as they had been socially prohibited from marriage or childbearing because of their rapes. In other words, becoming martyrs and suicide bombers was the only acceptable way to contribute to society and not be a disgrace to their society.[55]

Within Boko Haram, there has been an emerging trend of kidnapping women and forcing them into enlistment. Boko Haram's ideology exempts Muslim women from combat roles within the organization, though it is documented that this exemption is being relaxed and women are beginning to step into the line of fire more often.[56] In contrast though, Boko Haram's ideology says nothing about the Christian women that

---

[52] Bloom, 235.

[53] Bloom, 235.

[54] Bloom, 236.

[55] Karla J. Cunningham, "Cross-Regional Trends in Female Terrorism," *Studies in Conflict & Terrorism* 26, no. 3 (2003): 180, https://doi.org/10.1080/10576100390211419.

[56] Zenn and Pearson, "Women, Gender and the Evolving Tactics of Boko Haram," 10.

members abduct, who, at least in the early years of the organization, have been suspected of being used for all of Boko Haram's female suicide bombings.[57] It is of note that that organization has grown and evolved throughout the years and more women organic to the organization, meaning those who were not recruited through kidnapping, have begun to volunteer for suicide missions. Abductions of women have become a semi-official tactic within the Boko Haram organization since 2012 and have contributed considerably to the enlistment of non-voluntary participants and the roles that they are forced to play.[58]

C.   POTENTIAL EXPLANATIONS AND HYPOTHESES

Based on the examined literature, several hypotheses have emerged in order to explain the use of women within Boko Haram that are unique to this organization. In addition, recruitment tactics and enlistment motivations for women are being used more prevalently than documented in the past century. Three hypotheses will shed light on why and how Boko Haram is setting itself apart from its historic, cross-regional counterparts and how it is following in their historic trends:

Hypothesis 1: Based on existing knowledge of how women are used in extremist organizations, it is highly likely that Boko Haram is deviating from the trends and is using women as pawns and bargaining chips in order to gain leverage over their opposition and to create shock value in the media.

The first hypothesis assumes that women are being kidnapped and forced to participate as pawns in a larger, men's organization. Since resurgence in 2009, Boko Haram has carried out a series of kidnappings that would soon marked a new tactic and norm for this organization. Boko Haram's leader, Abubakar Shekau issued a statement following a particularly bloody and prolonged attack promising "to make these hostages his 'servants' if certain conditions, such as the release of Boko Haram members and their wives from prison, were not met."[59] Since then, kidnappings have become a common tactic for Boko Haram both for political and pragmatic reasons. This hypothesis does not

---

[57] Skinner, "The Rising Trend of Female Suicide Bombers in Nigeria," 2.

[58] Zenn and Pearson, "Women, Gender and the Evolving Tactics of Boko Haram," 52.

[59] Zenn and Pearson, 48.

encompass the entire spectrum of motivations that have been recorded for women within Boko Haram and does not take into consideration the voluntary enlistment of these participants.

Hypothesis 2: Regarding enlistment into the organization, current scholarship notes that most women enlist voluntarily for combat intensive roles. It his highly likely that Boko Haram is using the women whom they have kidnapped and tortured (either physically or mentally) as their main method of gaining female soldiers for combat such roles as suicide bombers, which would be deviating from historical norms.

In the case of suicide bombing, for example, it is a theorized that women are less likely to be suspected as suicide bombers and therefore have a higher chance of carrying out their mission.[60] Women who appear pregnant are seldom be stopped by security or law enforcement, and women seeking shelter at internally displaced person (IDP) camps are often not searched due to lack of suspicion or out of modesty.[61] In order to maximize utility of women and capitalize on their unique skills and circumstances, women are strategically being recruited in order to support specific roles and missions. Throughout cross-regional organizations, the enlistment of women as suicide bombers is a common and successful, theme; however, the tactic of kidnapping and forcing women to become suicide bombers is unique to Boko Haram. Therefore, it unquestionably must be considered when assessing and creating a plan of action for combatting that organization.

Hypothesis 3: Regarding individual motivations for women to enlist in Boko Haram, existing literature agrees that many women are seeking increased equality and legitimacy within society; they view participation in political activism and increased involvement in Islamic extremist organizations as a means by which to achieve these ends.

The final hypothesis argues that women are using their organization's cause as a stepping stone toward increased equality and respect within their society. As discussed, female suicide bombers are considered role models within their societies, as they can

---

[60] Bloom, *Bombshell: Women and Terrorism*, 22.

[61] Bloom, 22.

create legitimacy and an increased cultural respect for women through their activism within extremist organizations.

D. RESEARCH DESIGN

This thesis compares the female component of three historical terrorist organizations—The Chechen Black Widows, Al-Qaeda in Iraq, and the Afghanistan Taliban, all which are Islamic extremist organizations, and two of which have heavily utilized women in their fighting forces through different means. The Afghanistan Taliban, however, did not utilize women in martyrdom until pressured to do so by its Pakistani counterparts. This seemingly contradictory example was chosen in order to establish a counter narrative within the realm of Islamic extremist organizations and show the spectrum of utilization of women within FTOs.

The thesis first establishes a background of female involvement and motivations within these three terrorist organizations in order to establish cross-regional similarities and differences, and then analyze these cross-regionally established themes and compare them to what the international community is seeing in the present day with Boko Haram. This comparison enables the reader to look at these case studies that have already been resolved and studied and have a better understanding of how to best combat and understand this current threat. In order to establish themes between similarities and differences, I analyze female involvement as well as motivations of female insurgents within Boko Haram by providing an analysis taken from a mixture of both academically published works as well as data taken from international news articles on the most recent activity.

E. THESIS OVERVIEW AND CHAPTER OUTLINE

This thesis is broken up into four chapters. The introduction provides a historical background and thus, structural foundation, of both female involvement in terrorism globally as well as the Boko Haram FTO. The introduction is followed by a chapter in which I establish trends and themes of female integration and motivations of both individuals and those recruiting them from three major terrorist organizations, which were chosen based on geographical location and Islamic extremist ties. These show that these trends and themes can be found globally and establish that even within extremist organizations of the same religion, a spectrum of utilization of women is present. This chapter includes a brief background for each terrorist organization, as it is not the focus of this thesis, but is essential to understanding the context of the terrorist organization. The third chapter of this thesis delves into the activities of female insurgents within Boko Haram, as well as its enlistment motivations. The conclusion analyzes Boko Haram against its other Islamic FTO counterparts. It analyzes findings and key points as well as provide recommendations on how to proceed with the pursuit of stability and peace within Boko Haram's declared caliphate.

II. CROSS-REGIONAL SHADOW CASES

Prior to analyzing how Boko Haram utilizes women, it is valuable to analyze how FTOs at large utilize women within their organizations. The following sections provide a background into the Chechen Black Widows, the women of the Afghani Taliban, and the women of Al-Qaeda. These three organizations yield examples of commonalities and disparities that transcend cultural boundaries and will provide a background as a basis of comparison for Boko Haram's utilization of women.

A. THE CHECHEN REBELS—THE BLACK WIDOWS

On June 7, 2000, Khava Barayeva and Luisa Magomadova drove a truck filled with explosives into the temporary headquarters of a Russian Special Forces detachment, injuring five and killing two people, and in turn opened the world's eyes to what would be one of the deadliest separatists groups to date.[62] Until this date, the Chechen rebels had not utilized suicide bombers in their fight against Russia, and women specifically had only engaged in supporting roles throughout the organization. The women in Chechnya who served in support of the Chechen Rebels during the second Chechen war provide a unique model for the integration of women into an extremist organization, as they share the Islamic religious affiliation and ideology of Boko Haram, Al-Qaeda, and the LTTE, but differ significantly in culture from their cross-regional counterparts. The Chechen Black Widows, as named by the Russian and international press, attained their name in the early 2000s and have since participated in over 70 percent of Chechnya's suicide bombing attacks, with a staggering 50 percent of those attacks being carried out solely by women.[63] With the most known resistance fighters of this war being the Chechen Black Widows, this section will focus on their contribution to their cause.

---

[62] Anne Speckhard and Khapta Akhmedova, *Black Widows: The Chechen Female Suicide Terrorists* (Tel Aviv: Jaffee Center for Strategic Studies: Tel Aviv University, 2006), 1, http://www.inss.org.il/ publication/black-widows-chechen-female-suicide-terrorists/?offset=0&posts=1&type=405&outher=Anne%20Speckhard.

[63] Robert W. Kurz and Charles K. Bartles, "Chechen Suicide Bombers," *The Journal of Slavic Military Studies* 20, no. 4 (2007): 533, https://doi.org/10.1080/13518040701703070.

Support for suicide bombings is a new phenomenon in Chechen culture.[64] Kurz and Bartles explain, "the majority of the Chechen population does not believe that suicide bombers further the well-being of the community. Most Chechens deplore the practice and favor peace over the violent pursuit of national independence. Videos of suicide missions in Chechnya, for example, are not distributed to the Chechen population."[65] Yet, Chechen women were the first females to engage in religious terrorism in a combatant role.[66] While they paved the way for other Muslim women to participate in jihad, they first and foremost shocked the international community with just how far these women were willing to go to support their cause.

1.   Background

In order to understand the first, and ongoing second Russo-Chechen conflict it is best to understand the history between the Russian and the Caucasus Region, specifically Chechnya. Though the Chechen people have been identified as distinct from their Russian neighbors since the 17th century, they were subjected to Russian rule and Bolshevik occupation since the Russian Revolution in 1917. During World War II, Chechen and Ingush units collaborated with Nazi Germans, and consequently in 1944 Joseph Stalin deported between an estimated 400,000 to 800,000 Chechen nationals to Central Asia. Though repatriated in 1956 following the death of Stalin, Chechen citizens have not forgotten their forced exodus from their homeland. Upon the collapse of the Soviet Union in 1991, many states within the Caucasus Region pushed for independence from their regional-hegemon, Russia. Chechnya was no exception, and for possible geopolitical or economic reasons, was not granted independence from Russia and was instead met with an occupation of Russian troops. This led to the first Russo-Chechen conflict, which lasted from 1994 to 1996 and ended with Russian and Chechen officials

---

[64] Anne Speckhard and Khapta Akhmedova, "The Making of a Martyr: Chechen Suicide Terrorism," *Studies in Conflict & Terrorism* 29, no. 5 (September 22, 2006): 440, https://doi.org/10.1080/10576100600698550; Kurz and Bartles, "Chechen Suicide Bombers," 535.

[65] Kurz and Bartles, "Chechen Suicide Bombers," 535.

[66] Cindy D. Ness, *Female Terrorism and Militancy: Agency, Utility, and Organization* (New York, N.Y.: Routledge, 2008), 19.

signing a peace agreement in Dagestan.[67] With this historical tension ripe with conflict, unwanted occupation and unrecognized sovereignty, the stage was prime for another conflict and consequently the second Russian-Chechen conflict broke out in 1999.

In the three years following the first Chechen war, militant groups gained strength and notoriety among both the Chechen people, and the Russian authority. The terrain in Chechnya is vastly diverse, with plains in the north, woodlands in central Chechnya near the capital of Grozny, and treacherous mountains in the southern half.[68] In the wake of Aslan Maskhadov's election as president in 1997 though, this southern region became home to guerrilla fighters, who could easily store ammunition and weaponry, carry out elaborate ambushes of Russian forces, as well as move almost seamlessly between surrounding Georgia, Dagestan, and Ingushetia where safe havens had been established for insurgent forces.[69] Russian President Vladimir Putin refers to the second Chechen conflict as an "anti-terrorist operation,"[70] considering that all public order and discipline had broken down after the first conflict and was never reestablished by elected president, Aslan Maskhadov.[71] Under the pressure of Islamic extremists, he established strict sharia law throughout Chechnya in February 1999.[72] This pressure from both extremist organizations and the Russian government produced a volatile political environment and an environment that could not be sustained for very long without conflict.

Shamil' Basaev, a young warlord and losing presidential opponent to Maskhadov had gained the support of groups of "professional Islamists" who had been "trained in the Peshawar camps and commanded by Ibn al-Khattab, a jihadist who had fought earlier in

---

[67] Mark Kramer, "Guerrilla Warfare, Counterinsurgency and Terrorism in Teh North Caucasus: The Military Dimension of the Russian - Chechen Conflict," *Europe-Asia Studies* 57, no. 2 (2005): 209, https://doi.org/10.1080/09668130500051833.

[68] Kramer, 210.

[69] Kramer, 210.

[70] Thomas de Waal, "Analysis: Chechnya's Endless War," BBC News, April 23, 2001, http://news.bbc.co.uk/2/hi/europe/1292799.stm.

[71] Kramer, "Guerrilla Warfare, Counterinsurgency and Terrorism in Teh North Caucasus: The Military Dimension of the Russian - Chechen Conflict," 210–11.

[72] Kramer, 212.

Tadjikistan and Afghanistan."[73] These groups carried out attacks in defiance of the Russian government's hold on Chechnya as well as the rule of President Maskhadov, but never gained much traction in the media. The relative obscurity of these attacks is partially attributable to the rural and remote locations where they took place in relation to the rest of the world, as well as with the overshadowing of Russia's power. As a result, the international media was slow to pick up on the struggles of the Islamic extremists within Chechnya.[74] Chechen rebels resorted to more extreme methods of violence, not only to disrupt the domestic government and repel the perceived Russian occupation, but to gain international media attention as well.

2.   Tactics

Since mid-2000, Chechen rebels have focused on four types of attacks against the Russians as well as the Chechen government, which they saw as appeasing the perceived Russian occupation. These attacks began strictly with targeting the Russian military. Mark Kramer outlines these attacks as targeting: (1) Convoys, groups, and facilities of Russian troops and administrative personnel; (2) Russian military helicopters and aircraft; (3) individual Russian soldiers; and (4) officials and buildings associated with the pro-Russian Chechen government that was installed by Russian forces in mid-2000.[75] When these tactics did not produce the desired outcome, Chechen rebels extended attacks outside domestic borders and from strictly military to generalized civilian targets.[76] Kramer continues his outline of tactics outside of the Northern Caucasus, where "Chechen rebels have focused mainly on (1) crowds of civilians in Moscow and elsewhere; (2) key transport systems and government buildings; and (3) other civilian 'soft' targets."[77] Through the execution of these high profile attacks, Chechen rebels are

---

[73] Gilles Kepel, *Jihad: The Trail of Political Islam*, trans. Anthony Roberts (Cambridge, MA: The Belknap Press of Harvard University Press, 2002), 233.

[74] Kepel, 233.

[75] Kramer, "Guerrilla Warfare, Counterinsurgency and Terrorism in Teh North Caucasus: The Military Dimension of the Russian - Chechen Conflict," 216.

[76] Speckhard and Akhmedova, "The Making of a Martyr: Chechen Suicide Terrorism," 440.

[77] Kramer, "Guerrilla Warfare, Counterinsurgency and Terrorism in Teh North Caucasus: The Military Dimension of the Russian - Chechen Conflict," 216.

able to guarantee political and media attention. Women at the forefront of these attacks increased both shock value and interest.

Since the beginning of the second Chechen conflict, it has been evident that the Chechen rebels were willing to utilize women within their ranks without regard or need for fatwas.[78] This willingness stands outside the norm of many Islamic extremist organizations as most of these organizations such as the Afghan Taliban, for religious or cultural reasons, do not include their women in combatant roles unless it is absolutely necessary.

Karla Cunningham reported in 2008 that, "Since 2000, there have been 112 suicide terrorists, of whom forty-eight were women (43 percent) and sixty-four were men (57 percent). Women have been involved with 81 percent of the total suicide attacks involving Chechen rebels, and men working alone have carried out only 18 percent of the attacks."[79] This adoption of women by the Chechen rebels immediately into the ranks traditionally reserved for men is likely the result of how 'modern and westernized' they were prior to conflict. As Cindy Ness describes, women were made to keep "with former Soviet gender policies that emphasized female education and employment."[80] Ness further explains that "Chechnya's turn to Wahhabism, fanned by Arab mercenaries, appears to be more the product of political compromise to secure funding than of a Chechen commitment to Islamic belief."[81] Therefore, it is most likely that the blend of increased nationalism and religious ideology allowed for the utilization of women from the beginning of the second Chechen conflict. Knowing that within the history of Chechnya's struggle with a perceived oppression by Russia they were not getting the international media attention desired to raise awareness of their occupation, it is no surprise that from the start, Chechen rebels attacked with a strategy that would gather the most attention.

---

[78] Speckhard and Akhmedova, "The Making of a Martyr: Chechen Suicide Terrorism," 484.

[79] Ness, *Female Terrorism and Militancy: Agency, Utility, and Organization*, 91.

[80] Ness, 91.

[81] Ness, 91.

The Chechen Black Widows provide insight into how intense a culture of revenge coupled with religious backing and a heightened sense of nationalism can have on a conflict. The circumstances leading to the martyrdom of women within Chechnya drove them to become one of the most well-known and deadly groups of terrorist women that history has seen. According to Speckhard and Akhmedova,

> [prior] to the war, Chechen women had enjoyed more freedoms and occupational choices than women within ... other [Islamic extremist] groups perhaps lending to their immediate unfettered inclusion as bombers on par with the men. Likewise, as more men were killed and missing from their families, Chechen women were increasingly free to take on the culturally assigned role of avenging their deaths.[82]

While the Chechen rebels' more liberalized, secular stance on the incorporation of women on the frontlines is more progressive than their Islamic FTO counterparts, their ideology is similar to that of Al-Qaeda and other global jihadi groups, just focused on a nationalistic level.[83]

3. Motivations

The first and arguably most notable characteristic that can be found similarly throughout the Black Widow's international counterparts were their motivations—notably revenge. Robert Kurz and Charles Bartles state that, "in nearly all cases, Chechen suicide bombers did not broadcast their intentions beforehand or make statements on behalf of Islam and their people, suggesting that religious zeal and/or martyrdom is not the primary motivation used by most suicide recruiters in Chechnya. In many cases, the underlying motivation—particularly for female suicide bombers—is revenge."[84] Traditionally, Chechens live by a cultural ethos that designates the responsibility of avenging the death of a loved one to the family members.[85] This concept of direct

---

[82] Speckhard and Akhmedova, "The Making of a Martyr: Chechen Suicide Terrorism," 484.

[83] Speckhard and Akhmedova, 483.

[84] Kurz and Bartles, "Chechen Suicide Bombers," 532–33.

[85] Speckhard and Akhmedova, *Black Widows: The Chechen Female Suicide Terrorists*, 67.

revenge enacted solely upon the wrongdoer has expanded in a wartime era to revenge on those who were not directly responsible for the wrongdoing.[86]

Revenge has been cited as one of the largest influencers and motivators for female enlistment in extremist organizations, whether it is to avenge the death of a close family member or retaliate for past wrongs committed against the woman herself.[87] This wave of hatred and the need for revenge coupled with external Wahabbi ideologies adopted from well-established Afghan and Al Qaeda groups encouraged the Chechen population's acceptance and overall encouragement of suicide terrorism.[88] In December 2003, Chechen rebel leader Abu al-Walid al-Ghamidi stated,

> As you have seen and noticed, most of the suicide attacks were carried out by women… these women, particularly the wives of the mujahedin who were martyred, are being threatened in their homes, their honor and everything are being threatened. They do not accept being humiliated and living under occupation.[89]

The women among the Chechen rebels had mandated cultural norms that dictated a duty to avenge the death of a family member. This instilled duty led to a deep-rooted hatred and drive for revenge consequently making them the perfect candidates for martyrdom.[90]

In conjunction with or related to Chechen women's perceived need for revenge are the personal traumas that they have endured, whether that be the death or torture of a loved one, or sexual violence enacted upon them. Anne Speckhard writes that, in regards to studies conducted on the Black Widow's motivations:

> as far as we could discern, none of the Chechen suicide bombers in our sample had a serious personality disorder prior to deciding to join a terror group. No less important however, is that all individuals within the sample had experienced deep personal traumatization, and evidence of symptoms

---

[86] Speckhard and Akhmedova, 67.

[87] Bloom, *Bombshell: Women and Terrorism*, 235.

[88] Speckhard and Akhmedova, "The Making of a Martyr: Chechen Suicide Terrorism," 440.

[89] Robert A. Pape, *Dying to Win: The Strategic Logic of Suicide Terrorism* (New York: Random House Trade Paperbacks, 2006), 31–32.

[90] Kurz and Bartles, "Chechen Suicide Bombers," 534.

of post-traumatic stress disorder and dissociative phenomena as a result of direct personal traumatization were present in the entire sample.[91]

In addition to a personal need for revenge, the Black Widows show the desire for political activism and a strongly instilled sense of nationalism. The Black Widows exemplify a motivational linkage between political activism, religion, and personal revenge. David Cook explains that, "to date, women fighting in jihad have only been a factor in these nationalistic-Islamic resistance movements [Palestinian and Chechen], but not in other globalist radical Muslim warfare"[92] The Chechen rebels were quick to utilize women from the beginning of conflict, which can be theorized as an outcome of their "modernized" stance on gender policies, education and employment stances for women.[93] The combatant role of women in political and nationalistic violence is most frequently seen as being associated with leftist movements. Ness explains, "[B]y their very nature, left-wing groups are ideologically more suited to justify and advocate women assuming combatant and other non-traditional roles because they premise that fundamental problems in the political and social institutions of society require a radical break with the past."[94] The increased involvement of women in both combatant and non-combatant roles within the Chechen conflict provides insight on the enthusiastic use of women within an Islamic extremist organization, under the guise of nationalistic and revenge motivations.

B.   AL QAEDA—THE FEMALE JIHAD

In the wake of September 11, 2001, the largest threat to the United States has been terrorist threats that subscribe to the "Global Jihad movement."[95] The Salafiya-Jihadia movement evolved during the 20th century and is an offshoot of Salafi

---

[91] Speckhard and Akhmedova, *Black Widows: The Chechen Female Suicide Terrorists*, 66.

[92] Ness, *Female Terrorism and Militancy: Agency, Utility, and Organization*, 84.

[93] Ness, 84, 91.

[94] Ness, 84.

[95] Rohan Gunaratna and Aviv Oreg, "Al Qaeda's Organizational Structure and Its Evolution," *Studies in Conflict & Terrorism* 33, no. 12 (November 20, 2010): 1047, https://doi.org/10.1080/1057610X.2010.523860.

ideology.[96] Though this movement is global and has branches and influence on almost every continent, Al-Qaeda stands firmly in its fundamentalist beliefs and shows that while cultural influences can impact associated "branch" affiliates, the core of Al-Qaeda only began to utilize women in accordance with its beliefs when absolutely necessary and with no other option.

1.   Background

Unlike the Chechen rebels, Al-Qaeda is more of an ideology and international jihad with many affiliated organizations and networks than a centralized extremist organization within one, or a few countries. Also, unlike many Islamic extremist organizations throughout the world, Al-Qaeda poses a direct threat to the United States, and therefore has warranted significant domestic as well as international political and media attention since the terror attacks of September 11, 2001. Conceptualized by Palestinian religious cleric Abdullah Azzam in 1987 and founded by Osama bin Laden in the late stages of the Soviet-Afghan war in 1988, Al-Qaeda has had a role in countless terrorist attacks worldwide. Its goal is to wage a global jihad under three doctrinal tenets: "to unite the world's Muslim population under sharia; to liberate the 'holy lands' from the 'Zionist-Crusader' alliance, and to alleviate perceived economic and social injustices."[97] Though its associated organizations have begun incorporating women in their ranks, Al-Qaeda proper (i.e., the core segments of the extremist organization) has yet to utilize women in combatant roles, and has contained them to supporting functions only.[98]

Based in Afghanistan and Pakistan, Al-Qaeda is today led by Ayman al-Zawahiri and his top aides.[99] The complexity in combating Al-Qaeda, and a major contribution to its growth and success, is that it is a hybrid between a hierarchical structured organization

---

[96] Gunaratna and Oreg, 1047.

[97] Rohan Gunaratna and Aviv Oreg, "Al Qaeda's Organizational Structure and Its Evolution," *Studies in Conflict & Terrorism* 33, no. 12 (November 20, 2010): 1047, https://doi.org/10.1080/1057610X.2010.523860.

[98] Ness, *Female Terrorism and Militancy: Agency, Utility, and Organization*, 6.

[99] "Al-Qaeda," 3.

and a network structured terrorist organization. This structure is advantageous to the al Qaeda organization as it allows for cells to form and operate through the facilitation of the internet and without necessarily meeting in person.[100] Additionally, it allows for this organization to conduct complex tasks requiring extensive coordination and professional training and allows the organization to grow extensively and have global influence and recruitment. By operating as a network structured organization, Al-Qaeda is able to recruit and promote a jihadist ideology across all regions of the world, and, when necessary, revert back to the more efficient hierarchical structure. Rohan Gunaratna explains that Al-Qaeda is

> characterized by a broad-based ideology, a novel structure, a robust capacity for regeneration and a very diverse membership that cuts across ethnic, class and national boundaries. It is neither a single group nor a coalition of groups: it comprised a core base or bases in Afghanistan, satellite terrorist cells worldwide, a conglomerate of Islamist political parties, and other largely independent terrorist groups that it draws on for offensive actions and other responsibilities.[101]

Burke describes how, at ideological conception, Azzam "envisaged men who, acting independently would set an example for the rest of the Islamic world and thus galvanize the umma (global community of believers) against its oppressors."[102] This organizational structure based globally and on a jihad ideology has allowed for Al-Qaeda to grow into one of the most dangerous and deadly extremist organizations in the world.

2.   Tactics

The approach that Al-Qaeda has taken regarding the incorporation of women is multifaceted and women's integration is on the rise. Although organizations associated with Al-Qaeda have integrated women into their combatant ranks out of necessity, Al-Qaeda proper has been very reserved.[103] Ness explains that, "while al-Qaeda proper has

---

[100] Gunaratna and Oreg, "Al Qaeda's Organizational Structure and Its Evolution," 1045.

[101] Rohan Gunaratna, *Inside Al Qaeda: Global Network of Terror* (New York, N.Y.: Cambridge University Press, 2002), 54.

[102] Jason Burke, "Al Qaeda," *Foreign Policy,* 142 (June 2004): 18.

[103] Ness, *Female Terrorism and Militancy: Agency, Utility, and Organization,* 6.

been rumored to be training squads of women to engage in violent jihad since 9/11, to date it is not known to have dispatched any females on a suicide mission."[104] Women participating in this global jihad primarily fill the roles of facilitators, supporters, educators and recruiters.[105]

Al-Qaeda was extremely reluctant to integrate women into any combative roles until absolutely necessary. Anne Speckhard explains that, "Al Qaeda in Iraq was similar to the Palestinians, only equipping women for suicide missions when they became desperate in the face of enhanced security. Knowing that women in burqas could still breach checkpoints to carry out attacks, the group began to send them in droves."[106] This aversion to their direct usage in combat does not, though, depict the utilization of women within the organization as a whole. Women are increasingly being recruited by Al-Qaeda through the internet, as it places them on equal footing with their male counterparts, in spite of the conservative nature of the societies in which they live.

Six fatawa have been issued allowing women to participate in martyrdom operations. These fatawa have been issued by Yussuf al Qaradawi, three by the faculty at al-Azhar University Egypt, Faysal al-Mawlawi of the European Council for Research and Legal Opinion based in Dublin, and Nizar Abd al-Qadir Riyyam of the Islamic University of Gaza and explicitly dictate the role of women within this global jihad. Osama bin Laden states in the fatawa, "Declaration of War Against the Americans Occupying the Land of the Two Holy Places" that:

> Our women had set a tremendous example for generosity in the cause of Allah; they motivate and encourage their sons, brothers and husbands to fight for the cause of Allah in Afghanistan, Bosnia-Herzegovina, Chechnya and in other countries. (...) May Allah strengthen the belief—Imaan—of our women in the way of generosity and sacrifice for the supremacy of the word of Allah. (...) Our women instigate their brothers

---

[104] Ness, 6.

[105] Von Knop, "The Female Jihad: Al Qaeda's Women," 411.

[106] Anne Speckhard, "Female Terrorists in ISIS, Al Qaeda and 21rst Century Terrorism," Trends Research: Inside the Mind of a Jihadist, May 2015, 5, http://trendsinstitution.org/wp-content/uploads/2015/05/Female-Terrorists-in-ISIS-al-Qaeda-and-21rst-Century-Terrorism-Dr.-Anne-Speckhard.pdf.

to fight in the cause of Allah. (…) Our women encourage Jihad saying: Prepare yourself like struggler; the matter is bigger than the words.[107]

Within these fatawa, women are encouraged to take an active role in the jihad through enabling the men in their lives, and thus placing them in supporting roles.

Al-Qaeda (proper and associated) have utilized women heavily in supporting roles since its inception. This integration has played a vitally important role in both the short and long-term survival of the organization.[108] Women are the educators of the Al-Qaeda youth; they are tasked with raising them and teaching them the jihadi ideology. Von Knop explains that, "having 8, 10, or 12 children and educating them to become a Shahid is the Jihad of a mother."[109] The women of Al-Qaeda are utilizing their influence within their communities, and most importantly, in their families to recruit and raise the current and future generations of jihadi soldiers, whether this be through networking via the internet or in social and familial settings. Women have also proven to be highly effective recruiters to the jihad. Malika al Aroud, for example, was a Belgian woman who used a website that attempted to shame men into joining the global jihad.[110] She explained in her 2008 *New York Times* interview, "it's not my role to set off bombs—that's ridiculous … I have a weapon. It's to write. It's to speak out. That's my jihad. You can do many things with words. Writing is also a bomb."[111] The utilization of women in promoting Al-Qaeda's jihadi ideology and global recruiting campaign is a softer, more inviting approach that allows for the organization to reach out and bring in a wider, more diverse group of Muslims into the fold.

3.   Motivations

The women who are influenced by and being utilized in the Al-Qaeda organization are doing so in the name of religious jihad. Due to the Al-Qaeda's global

---

107 Von Knop, "The Female Jihad: Al Qaeda's Women," 406.

108 Von Knop, 409.

109 Von Knop, 410.

110 Speckhard, "Female Terrorists in ISIS, Al Qaeda and 21rst Century Terrorism," 6.

111 Elaine Sciolino and Souad Mekhennet, "Al-Qaeda Warrior Uses Internet to Rally Women," *New York Times*, May 28, 2008.

nature, it is likely that though underlying motivations may have nationalistic tones, the core motivations lay within religion. Women are heavily involved in recruitment of future Al-Qaeda soldiers. European intelligence officials have noted that there is an increase in the utilization of women within Al-Qaeda. While there is a rise in female suicide bombers, women's roles are still predominantly support-based. Intelligence officials still recognize that women hold just as deadly a role as "organizers, proselytizers, teachers, translators and fundraisers who either join their husbands in the fight or step into the breach as men are jailed or killed."[112] Social media and the internet are strong tools for global recruitment of Al-Qaeda members, and in particular, women. Impressionable young women around the world are lured in via flashy online magazines, articles, and conversations with members who glorify female roles in the jihad. This promise of a global jihad against the Western world and the rhetoric that—according to Abdallah Azzam—"jihad is every man's duty (fard ayn) wherever Muslim lands are occupied by foreigners"[113] By capitalizing on religious duty, women are lured into supporting roles within Al-Qaeda around the world.

C.   THE AFGHAN TALIBAN—THE FEMALE COMPONENT

In stark contrast to the Chechen Rebels and Al-Qaeda, the Afghanistan Taliban uses women in combatant roles in a very limited capacity, and with very limited publication and vocalization on its use of women. Members of the Taliban are experts of their own terrain and populations within it. They have proven to be sophisticated in their ability to adapt and innovate on the battlefield in order to most effectively combat their adversaries. Yet though they have mastered the ability to adapt and overcome the occupation challenges that they have faced within their Afghanistan homeland, they have been extremely reluctant to utilize women within combat and martyrdom roles, thus emphasizing the spectrum of roles and engagement of women within Islamic extremist organizations globally. By capitalizing on the cultural sensitivity though that comes with being a woman or child within Afghanistan, the incorporation of Pakistani Taliban

---

112 Sciolino and Mekhennet.

113 Kepel, *Jihad: The Trail of Political Islam*, 318.

suicide bombing methods has led to the deployment of women and children into this method of martyrdom. This allows for insurgents to more easily bypass security measures and enter the busiest areas without question or scrutiny, thus creating the largest casualty count possible.

1.   Background

Coming to prominence in late 1994, the Islamic Emirate of Afghanistan (IEA), more commonly are known as the Afghanistan Taliban, bears considerable similarities to its Islamic FTO counterparts. Similar to the Chechen Rebels, the Taliban came into existence with a message and campaign to expel Western influence from its country. Originating as an Afghanistan sect of the Pakistan Taliban who emerged in the early 1990s, the Afghani sect promoted a message of being the protectors of Islam and the only legitimate authority within Afghanistan.[114] The emergence of the Taliban can be attributed to three factors:

> first, the lack of state-building and inability of the Afghan government...; second, the failure to secure and stabilize the rural areas of the country so that development and reconstruction can proceed, and; third, the lack of any significant material improvement in the lives of most Pashtuns in the south and east of the country since the demise of the Taliban regime.[115]

Established out of perceived necessity to rid its nation of unwanted Western presence, the Afghanistan Taliban has successfully manipulated Islamic rhetoric in attempt to destabilize its U.S.-supported Kabul government and implement Shar'iah law.[116]

In the aftermath of the fall of Kabul in April of 1992 to the local mujahedeen, Afghanistan had fallen into a bloody anarchy.[117] In September of 1996, the Afghanistan

---

[114] Thomas H. Johnson, *Taliban Narratives: The Use and Power of Stories in the Afghanistan Conflict* (New York, N.Y.: Oxford University Press, 2017), 15–16; "Who Are the Taliban?," BBC News, May 26, 2016, http://www.bbc.com/news/world-south-asia-11451718.

[115] Thomas H. Johnson, "The Taliban Insurgency and an Analysis of Shabnamah (Night Letters)," *Small Wars & Insurgencies* 18, no. 3 (September 2007): 317–18, https://doi.org/10.1080/09592310701674176.

[116] Johnson, *Taliban Narratives: The Use and Power of Stories in the Afghanistan Conflict*, 16, 21.

[117] Kepel, *Jihad: The Trail of Political Islam*, 10–11.

Taliban retook power within Kabul, supported by both the United States and Pakistan and at the time funded by the Pakistani secret service (ISI). Though the Islamic religious ideology manifested in its most literal and ossified form, the Taliban provided stability and order in a country that had been subject to "four years of devastation, murder, rape, and pillage at the hands of the mujahedeen faction commanders."[118] This regime's early success and popularity was founded in its ability to bring law and order back to the people of Afghanistan, when corruption, lawlessness and unsolicited violence reigned.[119]

Once in power, the Afghani Taliban held its promise to instill peace and security through the implementation of Shar'iah law. At the core of its beliefs were six themes by which it ruled. Thomas Johnson explains:

- That Taliban victory in cosmic conflict is inevitable;

- That Islam cannot be defeated;

- That the Taliban are "national heroes" and willing to sacrifice all for Allah and country;

- That Afghans have a long and honorable history of defeating invading foreign infidels;

- That foreign invaders as well as their Afghan puppets are attempting to destroy Afghan religion and traditions;

- That all Afghans have an obligation to join the jihad against the foreigners and apostates.[120]

Though the Taliban remained firmly in power throughout Afghanistan, they extensively benefitted from United States and Saudi Arabian financial and management support, as they did not have either the competence or resources to do so without help.[121]

---

[118] Kepel, 11.

[119] "Who Are the Taliban?"

[120] Johnson, *Taliban Narratives: The Use and Power of Stories in the Afghanistan Conflict*, 21–22.

[121] Kepel, *Jihad: The Trail of Political Islam*, 12.

Without this support, the Afghanistan Taliban could rule and maintain power solely off the proceeds of contraband and opium.[122]

When the attacks on September 11, 2001, on the World Trade Centers in New York City and the Pentagon in Washington, DC, occurred, the Taliban and its regime came into the international spotlight. Not because they were credited with the attacks, but because it came to light that they had been providing safe haven as well as establishing effective partnership with both Osama Bin Laden and other key leadership of the Al-Qaeda organization in Afghanistan.[123] This international spotlight on the extremist rule of the Afghani Taliban and its implementation of Shar'iah law as well as its blatant deprivation of human rights to the women of Afghanistan led to the invasion of Afghanistan by American troops with a two-pronged approach. First, to overthrow the Taliban regime that United States government had previously supported, and secondly to find, capture, and kill Osama Bin Laden and other high-ranking Al-Qaeda officials responsible for the attack on American soil.

2. Tactics

Since the two occupations of Afghanistan—one by the Soviets from 1980 to 1989 and the other from US-NATO alliance between 2001 and 2011—the Taliban has been quick to modify tactics to most aptly suit its strengths and weaknesses.[124] The Taliban has found great success in utilizing both suicide bombers and IEDs, using tactics that its members learned and adapted from the Iraqi resistance. It also installed shadow government structures into Afghan provinces during the expansion of its organization in the early 2000s, and utilized the proven successful Shabnamah, or night letters, in order to spread its message and influence those that it is trying to control. These tactics allow members of the Taliban to know, understand, and connect with the local populations much more than the recognized government.

---

[122] Kepel, 12.

[123] Kepel, 13.

[124] Thomas H. Johnson, "Taliban Adaptations and Innovations," *Small Wars & Insurgencies* 24, no. 1 (2013): 3–4, https://doi.org/10.1080/09592318.2013.740228.

With the majority of research conducted being centered on the perceived oppression that women have faced at the hands of the Taliban insurgency, little quantitative data has been published providing hard numbers of support that women have provided to the Afghanistan Taliban. Dr. Rostami Povey, a researcher with the University of London, has conducted several field studies on women in Iran and the United Kingdom.[125] Her qualitative research shows that there was and still is a small minority of women who play supporting roles within the Taliban, whether that be within the expansive spy network, smuggling of weapons and messages, or by recruiting.[126] The research of journalist Terese Cristiansson reinforces this theory of supporting roles. She states that, "as Taliban wives they play a supporting but important role in the insurgency. Not only do they believe in the cause, but they also assist their husbands by smuggling weapons under their clothes, carrying messages and taking care of wounded fighters."[127] These women, though not in a combative role, have just as large of an impact on the organization as their combative counterparts.

Though women have not yet played a large combative role in the Taliban, it is clear that this organization has taken advantage of the cultural norms and utilized their female members in supporting roles to the fullest extent. These cultural guidelines have been outlined in part by Mary Anne Franks:

- Women may not work outside the home, except for a few health workers, or attend any kind of educational institution.

- Women are not allowed to leave their house at all unless accompanied by a mahram (a close male relative).

- Women are not allowed to be treated by male doctors.

---

[125] Seran de Leede, "Afghan Women and the Taliban: An Exploratory Assessment," in *ICCT Policy Brief* (Hague, Netherlands: International Centre for Counter-Terrorism - The Hague, 2014), 5, www.icct.nl.

[126] de Leede, 5–7.

[127] de Leede, 6.

- Women must wear a burqa (a garment that covers the body completely, with only a piece of mesh around the eyes) at all times.

- Women may not gather for any public functions or festivities.

- Women are not allowed to use cosmetics.

- The windows of women's houses must be painted over, so that women cannot be seen from the outside.

- Women must not talk or laugh loudly, must not wear high-heeled shoes or any shoes that make noise, must not wear bright colors, or at any moment allow any part of their flesh to show, wash clothes in public, or appear on the balcony of their houses, so as not to incite the lust of men.

- The names of places which include a reference to women must be changed; for example, "women's garden" is renamed "spring garden.[128]

Though these restrictions are commonly perceived as repressive by the international community, they are put into place under the guise of protection for the women, and conveniently provide a cultural cover to utilize women in the more active supporting roles of moving weapons and messages, and drugs.

Women in supporting roles play a less visible but invaluable role in the success of extremist organizations, in particular Afghanistan's Taliban. Cragin and Daly note that "logistics relate to the 'procurement, maintenance, and transportation of military material, facilities, and personnel; the handling of the details of an operation.' For terrorist or insurgent groups, logisticians smuggle weapons and funds to terrorist leaders and their operational cells."[129] Women recruiters are "individuals used or designated by terrorist leaders to attract new logisticians, financiers, suicide bombers, or guerrilla fighters into their organization. Recruiters also often serve as essential links between a terrorist or

---

[128] Mary Anne Franks, "Obscene Undersides: Women and Evil Between the Taliban and the United States," *Hypatia,* 18, no. 1 (Winter 2003): 139–40.

[129] Cragin and Daly, *Women as Terrorists: Mothers, Recruiters, and Martyrs*, 21.

insurgent group and popular support communities."[130] In integrating women into these supporting roles, the women are able to utilize the aforementioned cultural guidelines to their advantage in order to remain under the radar.

The assertion that the Taliban has and continues to actively recruit women is dubious. While it may be actively recruiting and forcing men into martyrdom, little to no evidence exists that the Taliban is approaching women for involvement in the same way.[131] Thomas Johnson explains how the Taliban has adopted shabnamah—or letters that are stuck onto walls of the masque or door of literate villagers at night for proclamation to the village the following day—into its repertoire for intimidation and undoubtedly indirect coercion of women into support.[132] He argues that,

The Taliban night letters represent a strategic and effective instrument, crafting poetic diatribes which appeal to the moral reasoning of Afghan villagers. While many of the night letters represent overt intimidation, they also present important insights into who and what the Taliban represents. The quality and use of these letters have impressed professional U.S. information and psychological (PSYOP) officers, who consider them 'eloquent and impressive' and subsequently more effective than the vast majority of U.S. information operation artefacts.[133]

The Taliban's night letters provide a connection with local populations that occupying forces will never be able to obtain. Night letters are generally plastered to the doors and walls of mosques and government buildings due to the fact that the majority of the population is illiterate.[134] Therefore, the Taliban relies on those that are educated to transmit the night letters.[135] The significance that these night letters render to the women of Afghanistan is the influence that they have through word of mouth. With the Afghan people being a tribal culture who put high emphasis on oral history and their families, the

---

[130] Cragin and Daly, 39.

[131] de Leede, "Afghan Women and the Taliban: An Exploratory Assessment," 7.

[132] Johnson, "The Taliban Insurgency and an Analysis of Shabnamah (Night Letters)," 320–21.

[133] Johnson, 321.

[134] Johnson, 321.

[135] Johnson, 321.

Taliban is easily able to capitalize on the literacy rates of the population and influence the narrative that is being told through night letters. Combining this tactic with a horizontal approach of influence—such as family members or friends—allows the Taliban to reach out and inadvertently influence women into supporting not only its cause, but to also become active participants in supporting roles.

Afghanistan's Taliban's utilization of women is not one that has entered into the combatant and martyrdom realm. Though little quantitative data is available to provide numbers, the qualitative research and studies have shown that women are not on the sidelines in the Taliban's fight against Afghanistan occupancy and that their roles within the organization should not be brushed aside. Women are still active participants in the supporting roles that they play, such as recruiters, spies and smugglers of firearms and messages. Though participation is known to be strictly voluntary, the influences of family and friends, as well as the subjection to a counter-Western narrative told through oral teachings and night letters inevitably plays a large role in painting Taliban objectives as enticing and religiously correct.

These three FTOs show the wide range of female utilization that is seen within Islamic extremist organizations globally. It is through these examples a foundation is laid for comparison and analysis to Boko Haram. This comparison will allow for accurate strategies and tactics to be recommended to the Nigerian and United States government on how to best combat the Boko Haram organization.

III. THE WOMEN OF BOKO HARAM

With an understanding provided by the Chechen Rebels, the Afghan Taliban, and Al-Qaeda of how women have been utilized within FTOs globally, an informed comparison can be made with Boko Haram. This chapter will provide a brief background of Boko Haram, how they utilize women, and the avenues by which women are integrated into the organization. This will provide the basis of understanding that is needed in order for the international community to better understand the unique differences that are seen in this FTO and ultimately combat this organization effectively.

A. CONTEXTUALIZED BACKGROUND

Boko Haram has significantly evolved in mission, motivation, and tactics since its inception in 2002. The conflict between Boko Haram and the Nigerian government within northeast Nigeria is complex, as it is deeply rooted in historical, political, economic, and ethnic dissension. McQuaid and Asfura-Heim argue that, "Boko Haram is a local, ethnic-based (Kanuri) revolutionary insurgent group which utilizes subversion, classic guerilla tactics, and terrorism to achieve its goals."[136] Boko Haram and its conflict within Northern Nigeria can be best analyzed by dividing it into two major timeframes, from 2002 to 2009 and from 2010 to present day. Boko Haram has evolved from a peaceful organization aimed at gaining more religious representation within the Nigerian government to a dangerous terrorist cell looking for retaliation and to overthrow and install an Islamic state within Nigeria.

1. Boko Haram from 2002 to 2009

At inception in 2002, Mohammed Yusuf's vision for Boko Haram was a peaceful, da'wa organization that aimed to bring awareness of the institutional inequality of the Nigerian government, as well as to preach religious secularism. The idea of da'wa, or

---

[136] Julia McQuaid and Patricio Asfura-Heim, "Rethinking the U.S. Approach to Boko Haram: The Case for a Regional Strategy," *CNA Analysis & Solutions*, February 2015, 8, https://www.cna.org/cna_files/pdf/DRM-2014-U-009462-Final.pdf.

"calling people to Islam" became a core duty for the organization.[137] Alexander Thurston explains that "by emphasizing da'wa, Boko haram sought to convince itself, other Salafis, and other Muslims that it had not abandoned global Salafism's missionary goal."[138] They aimed to change a government that has been perceived to have promoted economic inequality and religious misrepresentation between the northern and southern states. Though the group was formed in 2002, Boko Haram did not become its official name until 2010. The Kanuri people—who resided in the Borno province and converted to Islam centuries prior to their northern counterparts, the Hausas-Fulanis—saw themselves as the "rightful standard-bearers of Islam in Nigeria."[139] They have resided in the northeastern region of Nigeria since the territory was claimed by the Borno-Kanuri Empire who ruled this territory between 1380 and 1893.[140] As the Kanuri people were not only segregated along religious fault lines from the southern Christians in which conflict has erupted throughout the country between groups, they are also ethnically segregated from the Hausas-Fulani people residing in the northwestern region of the country. "The Kanuris…accuse the Hausa-Fulani leadership, and in particular the Sultan of Sokoto, of corruption and collusion with the Christian government."[141] It is with this narrative, and in response to the deep-rooted economic and religious instability within the northeastern, Borno region, that Mohammed Yusuf based the foundations of Boko Haram and its mission of gaining both legitimate and religious representation within the Nigerian government.

In the early years of Boko Haram, under Mohammed Yusuf's rule, public approval of the organization was extremely high. In an effort for purification that only became more radical as the organization grew, he preached what he considered to be an orthodox Islam, making a distinction between this religious interpretation and what he

---

[137] Alexander Thurston, *Boko Haram: The History of an African Jihadist Movement* (Princeton, New Jersey: Princeton University Press, 2018), 17.

[138] Thurston, 17.

[139] Asfura-Heim and McQuaid, "Diagnosing the Boko Haram Conflict: Grievances, Motivations, and Institutional Resilience in Northeast Nigeria," 9.

[140] Asfura-Heim and McQuaid, xiii.

[141] Asfura-Heim and McQuaid, 10.

considered to be anti-Islamic practices—democracy, constitutionalism, alliances with non-Muslims, and Western-style education.[142] After leaving the Indimi mosque of his teacher Ja'far Adam, because of ethnic differences between the Hausa patronage, Yusuf established his own mosque complex and began gathering a strong following of Kanuri people, as well as non-Kanuri immigrants to the city of Maiduguri.[143] Yusuf was predominantly accepted by both the Hausa and Kanuri communities as he preached in both languages, yet with Ja'far Adam being ethnically Hausa and Yusuf being Kanuri, many of the Kanuri attendees felt that they were being denied teaching and leadership positions within the mosque by the Hausa. This ultimately led to a cry for Yusuf to leave the Indimi mosque and preach in his own. Once in control of his own mosque, Yusuf began to rapidly gain political and popular control. This was propelled by the fact that he created an "imaginary state within a state, administering private justice and delivering social services."[144] Asfura-Heim and McQuaid explain, "Yusuf wanted to set up a state-like organization, operating initially on a small scale, parallel to the federal government. He believed that his organization would inevitably grow until it would replace the actual state."[145] The fact that he had a conservatively estimated constituency of "over five hundred people, and a wider audience of interested and sympathetic persons that might have reached ten thousand people" can be evidenced in the hagiographies following his death in 2009.[146] By appealing predominantly to the poor population as well as aligning himself with the political elite in Maiduguri, Yusuf placed himself in a prime position to accrue resources that he could then allocate to the severely economically disadvantaged.

On the one hand, the Nigerian economy is one of the fastest growing in the world; thus, it would seem counterintuitive that inequality and poverty remain so rampant. Yet population growth has vastly outpaced economic growth.[147] The population grew from

---

[142] Thurston, *Boko Haram: The History of an African Jihadist Movement*, 106.

[143] Thurston, 85–87.

[144] Thurston, 89.

[145] Asfura-Heim and McQuaid, "Diagnosing the Boko Haram Conflict: Grievances, Motivations, and Institutional Resilience in Northeast Nigeria," 29.

[146] Thurston, *Boko Haram: The History of an African Jihadist Movement*, 89.

[147] Thurston, 28–29.

"89 million in 1991 to over 140 million in 2006, to more than 180 million in 2016....As of 2016, 43 percent of the population was under the age of fifteen years; another 19 percent was under the age of twenty-five."[148] This rapid population growth coupled with weakening agricultural production that the northern states so heavily rely on, the poverty rate of the northeast rose from 35.6 percent to 72.4 percent between 1980 and 2006. This rise in poverty was second only to the northwestern states, where the poverty level reached 79.2 percent.[149] In comparison to the southern Nigerian states, with poverty rates averaging between 55.9 and 63.1 percent, this economic disparity is considerable.[150] This crippling inequality has led to distrust of the Nigerian government and thus the popularity of Mohammed Yusuf during his rise and his establishment of Boko Haram.[151]

Institutionalized corruption and the consequent economic disparity between the northern and southern Nigerian states laid the foundation for the ethnopolitical and religious exclusion within government that would drive Boko Haram from a peaceful organization based in Islamic fundamentalism to one of violent conflict following the death of Mohammed Yusuf in 2009. Philip Roessler defines political exclusion as entailing, "the barring or intentional non-appointment of representatives of a subset of the population from the central government."[152] This exclusion is evidenced in post-independence Nigeria, with its long road to state and political creation. Thurston explains that the regional political units, or states that Nigeria created, "were meant to give greater political [and ethnic] representation to constituencies that felt stifled by the major ethnic groups—the Hausa, Yoruba, and Igbo. In this way, authorities hoped to weaken smaller groups' calls for autonomy and secession. In practice, however, the new states became "arena [s] of exploitation" for local elites."[153] This elite manipulation of state-appropriated resources has resulted in the longstanding perceived inequality of the Kanuri

---

148 Thurston, 28–29.

149 Thurston, 29.

150 Thurston, 29.

151 Thurston, 29–31.

152 Philip Roessler, *Ethnic Politics and State Power in Africa: The Logic of the Coup-Civil War Trap* (Cambridge, UK: Cambridge University Press, 2016), 63.

153 Thurston, *Boko Haram: The History of an African Jihadist Movement*, 41.

people, and thus the formation of an organization that believed that it could take care of the ethnic population through its religious fundamental ideologies when the government was failing to do so.

2.   Boko Haram from 2009 to Present

In the violent encounter with police forces on 11 June 2009, Boko Haram leader Mohammed Yusuf was killed. Subsequently, the organization went underground for a year-long hiatus. During this time, and under the new leadership of Abubakar Shekau—one of Yusuf's previously more radical leaders—Boko Haram took the time to regroup and transform from a dawah (proselytization) movement into one that "sought to expel the northern political establishment and eventually, to overthrow the national government."[154] At this point, Boko Haram's days of public preaching and service were over. This newfound organization embraced targeted assassinations, deployment of improvised explosive devices, suicide bombings, and the kidnapping and hostage taking of all ages and genders of people.[155] Abubakar Shekau neatly wrapped the expedited execution of Mohammed Yusuf into the narrative that Boko Haram was the victim of the Nigerian state. By killing of Mohammed Yusuf, the state had only eliminated the face of the organization; it had not addressed the driving factors and grievances that Boko Haram had been preaching. Consequently, the death of Yusuf further drove the extremist organization underground and fanned the embers of hatred and revenge into a full-blown flame.

In the days following the violent uprising and clash with Nigerian police, a Boko Haram spokesperson released this statement indicating the new era that this organization had entered into. He stated:

> We have started a Jihad in Nigeria which no force on earth can stop. The aim is to Islamize Nigeria and ensure the rule of the majority Muslims in the country. We will teach Nigeria a lesson, a very bitter one. ... From the month of August, we shall carry out series of bombings in Southern and

---

154 Asfura-Heim and McQuaid, "Diagnosing the Boko Haram Conflict: Grievances, Motivations, and Institutional Resilience in Northeast Nigeria," 26.

155 Asfura-Heim and McQuaid, 26.

Northern Nigerian cities, beginning with Lagos, Ibadan, Enugu and Port Harcourt. … We shall make the country ungovernable, kill and eliminate irresponsible political leaders of all leanings, hunt and gun down those who oppose the rule of Sharia in Nigeria and ensure that the infidel does not go unpunished.[156]

This transition to extremist violence would be evidenced in the series of terrorist attacks that would follow after Boko Haram's return in September 2010. The organization soon became known for surprise attacks on three main categories of people—members of security forces, Borno State politicians from the ruling All Nigeria People's Party (ANPP), and Muslim religious leaders who had publicly denounced the sect—with increasing severity and casualty counts and with the expectation that security responses would be slow.[157] These attacks produced the desired effect of eliciting fear from both the local population, providing coverage by domestic and international media, as well as finally gaining the attention of Nigerian government authorities as a credible threat that needed to be taken seriously.

In the years following Boko Haram's turn toward more extremist guerrilla tactics, the group was only too willing to take credit for the bombings of Christian churches and targeted attacks on religious leaders in an attempt to reignite the historical tensions between the northern Muslim community and the southern Christians.[158] The group's rhetoric became increasingly sharpened with its demand of the expulsion of Christians from the northern Nigerian states. In the early stages of this paradigm shift toward martyrdom, the victims of Boko Haram's violence excluded Muslim bystanders and were very targeted attacks, thus indicating the continued adherence to the original ideological foundations on which Mohammed Yusuf had based the organization. As years passed, a fundamental shift occurred within the global views of the group and its willingness to accept collateral damage during targeted violence, and attacks became indiscriminate. By 2014, Muslim victims themselves had become primary targets.[159] These Muslim victims

---

[156] Thurston, *Boko Haram: The History of an African Jihadist Movement*, 144.

[157] Thurston, 152–53.

[158] Thurston, 157.

[159] Thurston, 157.

represented a fundamental shift in ideology, from being a dawah movement to one focused on jihad, hatred, and revenge.

In present day it is difficult to determine a way to move forward in ending the conflict between Boko Haram and the Nigerian government. Boko Haram's demands of a split Nigerian state and the establishment of a completely Islamic state, to include the Christian dominated areas, seems unrealistic. Yet looking in hindsight at the timeline of this organization and the key turning points both in the early days of inception, as well as in 2009 and 2010 when the group was reorganizing and reestablishing itself, efforts could have been made by the federal government to mitigate the root causes. The weak state, deep rooted corruption, the carelessly heavy-handedness of the military response, and the failed attempt at power-sharing have only exacerbated the anger and revenge motives that drive Boko Haram members and only further the death count of innocent bystanders.

B.   UTILIZATION OF WOMEN

Boko Haram began integrating women into its combatant ranks during its reformation in 2010. Since its inception in 2002, the leaders of Boko Haram have preached acceptance of women and recruited them to join the organization. But not until its resurgence after the death of Mohammed Yusuf did women became actively utilized in martyrdom roles. Under the guise of being a vanguard for the interests of Muslim women, Boko Haram has utilized abductions and the psychological manipulation of these women in order to further its terror campaign in northern Nigeria. An International Crisis Group report explains women's importance to the organization. The group states:

> Women and girls' importance for Boko Haram stems from their roles and how they are perceived in society—both in the North East and in Nigeria as a whole. As wives, they enhance social status and provide sexual or domestic services (sometimes forced), thereby becoming valuable incentives for potential male recruits. Their adherence, willing or force, to the movement's version of Islam can also contribute to the spreading of its ideology among other women, but possibly also young men. Women can perform roles very different from traditional stereotypes. As the war

evolved, women have become recruiters, spies, domestic labor, fighters and forced or willing suicide bombers.[160]

By utilizing women in both supporting roles and combative roles, Boko Haram has become unequivocally effective in its utilization of women and is considered to be one of the deadliest terrorist organizations in history.

1.   Suicide Bombers and Fighters

Though female fighters are not the norm within Boko Haram, they are present throughout the organization. More prominent though is the use of female suicide bombers who have become an integral part of the organization and their campaign against the Nigerian government, and in the organization's quest to gain international recognition and legitimacy. Speckhard and Akhmedova explain that whenever traumatic experiences are widespread within areas that are repressed but still have a strong religious ideology present, several factors are commonly observed and provide ripe conditions for suicide terrorism. These factors include:

- Demonization of the enemy

- Promotion of jihad

- Cultural permission for extreme measures to be taken in conflict resolution

- Glorification of martyrdom where sacred values are perceived to be worth dying for

- Promises of an afterlife for martyrs

- Glorification of suffering and giving one's life for the community good[161]

Due to Boko Haram's increasing hatred for the Nigerian government and economic inequality throughout the country, women have become integral to its efforts to

---

160 International Crisis Group, *Nigeria: Women and the Boko Haram Insurgency*, 6.

161 Speckhard and Akhmedova, "The Making of a Martyr: Chechen Suicide Terrorism," 485.

gain international political and media attention with female suicide bombers being at the core of these tactics.

Regarding the use of female fighters, one top commander in the Civilian Joint Task Force (CJTF) within the Borno State explains that, "there are not many, but they are there. I have even seen one using an RPG [rocket-propelled grenade], … the women fighters are even more dangerous than the men fighters' because they seem even more fearless than their male counterparts."[162] It is seemingly common that the women used for fighting have been brought within the camp; they would start as sympathizers and volunteers and over time would be valued for their strength and dedication and would then be integrated into fighting forces. Women who become fighters, as opposed to suicide bombers, tend to be older than their male counterparts.[163] This age disparity is possibly because they seemingly must be integrated into the sect, trusted to carry out the mission and not run away, and then trained in the art of guerilla warfare prior to being utilized within the combatant ranks; whereas suicide bombers are much easier to train and equip for a one- time mission. An International Crisis Group report from 2016 explains:

> Unlike other West African insurgent groups, such as those in Liberia and Sierra Leone, Boko Haram has nothing like a women's brigade. Yet, under manpower pressure, particularly from 2014, some women and girls were trained and joined in attacks. The wife of a Boko Haram leader in the Gwoza Hills reportedly carried a gun and killed a vigilante. Armed female militants were sighted in the Sambisa forest, riding their own motorcycles. Women were said to be involved in a 2016 ambush on the military. On 10 July 2014, armed females between fourteen and 21 and fighting 'like professionals' attacked Kirenowa in Marte LGA, Borno state.[164]

Whether out of necessity or willingness, by utilizing women in combatant roles and not just as suicide bombers, Boko Haram is progressing into a modernized realm of warfare and stepping out of fundamentalist tactics. Though there are still not many

---

[162] Hilary Matfess, *Women and the War on Boko Haram: Wives, Weapons, Witnesses* (London, England: Zed Books, 2017), 131, http://www.zedbooks.net.

[163] Matfess, 131.

[164] International Crisis Group, *Nigeria: Women and the Boko Haram Insurgency*, 10.

women integrated into combatant roles, the few that are undoubtedly paving the way for increased numbers as the conflict continues.

Female suicide bombers have become symbolic of Boko Haram's brutality since its resurgence in 2010, with the first female suicide bomber attack being carried out in 2011.[165] Since women martyrs attract so much publicity and international attention, the organization has been one of the only extremist organizations to utilize them in its suicide bombing endeavors since what could be considered the beginning of its violent phase and what the majority of the world views as the conception of the organization. *Newsweek* reported in 2017 that Boko Haram, since April of 2011, has deployed 434 suicide bombers of which 244—or 56 percent—were female.[166] Gaffey explains that "the trend for women to be deployed is increasing, too: since the start of 2017, nearly two-thirds of Boko Haram's suicide attackers are female."[167]

Abubakar Shekau realized that there was great value in breaking gender norms in order to gain recognition with not only the Nigerian government, but also the international community. Matfess explains, "The symbolic value of using women as weapons, including the ability of this tactic to cultivate an aura of fear in local populations by upending gender norms and expectations, should not be underestimated."[168] As Andrew Walker notes, the "female suicide bombers contained a potent propaganda message: that Boko Haram is prepared to destroy the things the West holds most valuable."[169] Through the utilization of women as suicide bombers, Boko Haram knows that they can send a direct message to the international community that its martyrs could be anyone at any time. This sends a direct message that no person is safe from the organization and instills fear in the minds of the public, consequently giving them the recognition they strive for.

---

[165] International Crisis Group, 10.

[166] Conor Gaffey, "ISIS Just Started Using Female Suicide Bombers, but Boko Haram Has Been Doing It For Years - and Shows No Signs Of Stopping," *Newsweek*, August 12, 2017, http://www.newsweek.com/isis-boko-haram-nigeria-suicide-bomber-649790.

[167] Gaffey.

[168] Matfess, *Women and the War on Boko Haram: Wives, Weapons, Witnesses*, 133.

[169] Matfess, 133.

Female suicide bombing attacks grew exponentially in frequency in the latter half of 2014, mainly focusing on soft targets such as markets and bus stations within urban areas.[170] An International Crisis Group report states:

> The youngest female bomb-carriers are often victims themselves, with little awareness, duped by relatives and possibly drugged. But the older bombers seem to have volunteered. A woman who spent two years as a captive in Gwoza LGA said she saw seven such women who were recruited as suicide bombers and deployed to Maiduguri around March–April 2015. They reportedly were moved by commitment to jihad and apparently indoctrinated over a long period, including with promise of direct admission to al-Jinnah (paradise). Some were [also] widows of fighters.[171]

The utilization of female suicide bombers in fact has been so effective that male members of Boko Haram have reportedly been known to dress up as women in order to avoid detection and carry out their missions.[172] With heightened states of security in urban areas by the Nigerian government, it is exponentially easier for women to access more crowded venues and carry out their missions more effectively.

2. Wives and Breeders

Though Boko Haram extensively uses women as martyrs, the majority of women (both abducted and sympathizers) do not actively take part in combatant roles. The majority of women within Boko Haram stay within the camp and execute the day-to-day activities of keeping the camp running, including, but not limited to, the cooking, cleaning, and sexual requests of the men. These women who live and work within the camps fall into two main categories: the wives of soldiers and sympathizers and the slaves that refuse to conform. There are distinct differences between the wives of soldiers and the Boko Haram sympathizers, and the sexual slaves that are used purely to do manual labor around the camps and breed future soldiers for the organization. Though the wives of foot soldiers do not have all of the privileges that wives of the sect's leadership

---

[170] Matfess, 133; International Crisis Group, *Nigeria: Women and the Boko Haram Insurgency*, 10.

[171] International Crisis Group, *Nigeria: Women and the Boko Haram Insurgency*, 10–11.

[172] Zenn and Pearson, "Women, Gender and the Evolving Tactics of Boko Haram," 49.

do, they do still maintain a much healthier and happier lifestyle than that of those who refuse to conform.

The difference within the hierarchy of women is relatively major. The wives of sect leadership have servants who help them with their day-to-day activities as well as the most lavish weddings within the sect.[173] As well, women who are married to leaders within Boko Haram play a large role in managing and organizing the day-to-day functions and social services within the camp. For those women married to foot soldiers, the weddings are not as extravagant, nor are the privileges. They are mainly responsible (as are all wives) for child rearing and the running of the household, but in addition to this, these women are occasionally responsible for playing a supporting role to their husbands out in town. Matfess explains the roles of soldiers' wives:

> In addition to keeping house and rearing children, the wives of foot soldiers were also sometimes responsible for carrying their husband's weapons. This has two implications: first, the veil of ignorance adopted by many women about the sect's violent activities is, to some degree, a charade; and second, the reports from military and vigilante groups of women in conservative veils carrying weapons may not refer to female fighters, but rather to helpers of the soldiers.[174]

The lives of the women who are slaves or submissives, but not married to any male Boko Haram member, revolve around the maintaining Qur'anic education for other women, as well as the children, born into the organization and dress restrictions as well as bearing children for the insurgents. The ability to move between classifications of wife and slave or submissive is available. If enslaved women wish to become wives and have proven themselves through education and loyalty to the sect, they may be chosen to marry one of the soldiers and move up in class. Another defining positional marker for how wives are treated is what number wife they are to their husband and how many wives their husband has. Men with more wives tend to rank higher in the leadership chain, and their wives tend to be better cared for. Women who are married to men of higher stature tend to also rank higher in the organization against the other women. They

---

173 Matfess, *Women and the War on Boko Haram: Wives, Weapons, Witnesses*, 136–37.

174 Matfess, 138.

may not be required to do everyday chores, cook for the camp, or teach and raise the children.

Much like outside of the camps within many parts of Nigerian society, the lives of women married into Boko Haram revolve around child rearing and the growth of those children into either future wives or soldiers. Matfess explains, "according to the wives of insurgents, until their sons are old enough to be trained as soldiers and their daughters old enough to be married, it is the mother's responsibility to ensure that the child attends the sect's Qur'anic education and, when appropriate, public preaching."[175] The wives of Boko Haram soldiers are well taken care of medically when it comes to childbirth, as doctors are highly respected within the organization.[176]

Governor Kashim Shettima of Borno, who assumed office after the May 2011 elections, has explained that "members of Boko Haram 'have a certain spiritual conviction that any child they father will grow to inherit their ideology.'"[177] Because of this, whether through rape and forced impregnation or through voluntary conception, the men of Boko Haram actively seek to convert and recruit all women from towns that they raid into the organization to breed as many future soldiers as possible. Governor Shettima has noted that this is "procreation without responsibility" given the economic hardships that plague Northern Nigeria.[178]

C.   AVENUES OF RECRUITMENT

It is important to note, that though Boko Haram does use abduction as a major method for growth in ranks, many women willingly volunteer their services and lives to the organization. While it is appealing to paint all women within Boko Haram under the brush of helpless victims that would be inaccurate and deprive these women of what few freedoms they have in Nigerian society. Women within Nigerian society have, throughout history, faced systematic structural violence. This oppression blurs "the lines

---

[175] Matfess, 125.

[176] Matfess, 126.

[177] Matfess, 124.

[178] Matfess, 124.

of consent, coercion, autonomy and oppression...Women's limited opportunities, a result of repressive character of social and political norms, particularly in the north, may be seen as a coercive 'push factor,' encouraging female participation in the radical group."[179] Though the gender politics of the organization have changed, Boko Haram has always been, and continues to be, comparatively pro-woman when viewed against larger Nigerian social and political systems. Female support and recruitment to this organization fall under two categories, voluntary and involuntary.

1.   Voluntary Recruitment

Under Mohammed Yusuf, Boko Haram made the effort to "capitalize on the marginalization of women in order to garner their support."[180] The organization worked to provide Islamic education for women that was not readily available or prioritized. Ahmed-Ghosh argues,

> When questioning how women become involved with extreme religious groups the world over, it is important to understand that women 'may see religious movements as serving their own interests, interests which focus on maintaining the household and the community'. Particularly in sects with a group-help component, membership 'is not just a matter of religion, but also of an institution that is perceived as privileging them and providing the stability they need to survive.[181]

Yusuf believed that quality Islamic education allowed for women to properly raise the next generation. As women in Nigeria have been marginalized in their society nearly their entire lives, the access to education in any form provided an opportunity that was virtually unheard of. This access to Islamic education has been cited as a major contributing reason why women and girls subscribed to Yusuf's sect of Boko Haram in the early 2000s.[182]

Marriage into Boko Haram is a frequently utilized conduit for women to join and support the organization in order to gain relative security and freedom for themselves and

---

[179] Matfess, 103.

[180] Matfess, 56.

[181] Matfess, 57.

[182] Matfess, 57.

their extended families in comparison to conditions for women in general throughout Northern Nigeria.[183] As one internally displaced young woman recalled, "when Boko Haram entered her town 'some girls married the fighters willingly, some married for food, and some refused and were killed or beaten.'"[184] By voluntarily marrying into this organization, these women ensure that their basic needs are taken care of. One 18-year-old who was forcibly taken into Boko Haram explained that, "when you marry Boko Haram, you are free. All you have to do is clean a little."[185] In regions of harsh economic inequality and extreme poverty, this option is very popular. The International Crisis Group explains that, "In a village near Kerenowa in the Local Government Area (LGA) of Marte, Borno state, insurgents married 80 girls, offering dowries of 15,000 naira (about $70 in 2014), a considerable sum in a war-torn rural area."[186] By offering financial stability as well as a reliable source of food and education for its women, Boko Haram provides a tempting incentive for those women who are struggling in a war torn, repressive state. These women gain stability and security by willingly marrying into the organization, while Boko Haram gains women to birth and raise their children in the faith and to be fighters. Women who voluntarily convert to the sect and wed into the organization tend to be treated with more compassion and afforded more rights than those who are involuntarily recruited and resist forced assimilation.

2.   Involuntary Recruitment

The second source from which Boko Haram gains female recruits is through involuntary means. Boko Haram still uses abductions and manipulation not only as a significant method of sourcing the women needed to run the day to day operations within camps, but as a means of holding leverage and gaining retributions against the Nigerian government for the detention and deaths of its militants.[187] For women who live within towns and villages subject to Boko Haram raids, if they do not volunteer to marry into the

---

[183] Matfess, 105.

[184] Matfess, 105–6.

[185] Matfess, 105.

[186] International Crisis Group, *Nigeria: Women and the Boko Haram Insurgency*, 9.

[187] Matfess, *Women and the War on Boko Haram: Wives, Weapons, Witnesses*, 82.

organization, are forced into either domestic or sexual slavery from which they can then convert and assimilate or attempt freedom and risk extreme punishment if caught. Women who are abducted and do not willingly convert to Islam and join the organization are subjected to the much harsher treatment than those who volunteer to stay and join ranks.

> The abduction and subsequent treatment of women and girls constitute a gross abuse of human rights. Human Rights Watch summarized that abducted women and girls who refused to convert were killed or 'subjected to physical and psychological abuse; forced labor; forced participation in military operations, including carrying ammunition or luring men into ambush; forced marriage to their captors; and sexual abuse, including rape', in addition to the general demands placed on women 'to cook, clean, and perform other household chores.[188]

It would seem that in the interest of self-preservation, the best option for women who are abducted by Boko Haram would be to willingly convert and/or marry into the organization.

Throughout its tenure, Boko Haram continues to raid and kidnap women and children in order to gain tactical advantage over its adversaries by using them as leverage and revenge. According to Amnesty International, between 2014 and 2015 alone, Boko Haram kidnapped at least 2,000 women and girls and either forced them into sexual slavery or trained them to fight.[189] An International Crisis Group report from 2016 explains that "the seizure of more than 200 schoolgirls near Chibok in 2014 [is] a much publicized spike in a wider trend. The group took Christian and later Muslim females to hurt communities that opposed it, as a politically symbolic imposition of its will and as assets. By awarding "wives" to fighters, it attracted male recruits and incentivized combatants."[190] Boko Haram's motivations in abducting women is not only founded in the tactical and strategic fight against the perceived oppressive Nigerian government, but also in self-service of breeding future soldiers, growth from recruitment opportunities,

---

[188] Matfess, 88.

[189] "Nigeria: Abducted Women and Girls Forced to Join Boko Haram Attacks," Amnesty International, April 14, 2015, https://www.amnesty.org/en/latest/news/2015/04/nigeria-abducted-women-and-girls-forced-to-join-boko-haram-attacks/.

[190] International Crisis Group, *Nigeria: Women and the Boko Haram Insurgency*, i.

and maintaining the everyday function of insurgency camps.[191] Though the number of women known to belong within Boko Haram has grown exponentially in the years following its rebirth in 2009, it is difficult to calculate exactly how many women and girls have been kidnapped, how many willingly converted to the Islamic sect and how many joined the organization voluntarily as exact numbers are largely unknown.

---

[191] Matfess, *Women and the War on Boko Haram: Wives, Weapons, Witnesses*, 96.

THIS PAGE INTENTIONALLY LEFT BLANK

IV. ANALYSIS AND CONCLUSION

Having explored the background and analysis of four FTOs, it is now possible to analyze the similarities and differences as well as provide recommendations for a way forward in combating Boko Haram. This chapter will delineate the unique characteristics of Boko Haram in comparison to the Chechen Rebels, the Afghan Taliban, and Al-Qaeda. This allows for recommendations to both the Nigerian and United States government on best courses of action in the fight against this FTO.

A. ANALYSIS

When it comes to extremist organizations, each falls onto a spectrum of influence with religion and religious traditions on one end and cultural norms and influences on the other. Though religion plays a large role in many cultures it is a separate factor that transcends cultural boundaries. The comparison of Boko Haram to the Chechen Black Widows, Al-Qaeda, and The Afghanistan Taliban ultimately shows how each of these organizations, falls in wildly different ranges on this scale. While all four organizations are religiously Islamic and fundamentalist at their core, all are vastly different in their beliefs on how women should be utilized within the organization and in the fight. I believe these differences are rooted in the culture around which the organization was built. In the case of the Chechen Black Widows, the Chechen culture was one that fostered gender equality and the organization was formed in a more "westernized" light, thus fostering an environment for the utilization of women in combatant roles. Whereas in the Afghani Taliban, women were strictly used in supportive roles until the methods and tactics of the Pakistani Taliban began transcending borders and the implementation of women into combatant roles slowly increased out of necessity. Al-Qaeda takes a more middle-ground approach and utilizes women in both roles. Boko Haram runs somewhere in the middle of the culture vs. religious spectrum as well. Boko Haram has recognized the shock value and international attention that combative utilization of both kidnapped and volunteer women would bring to its organization, as well as the necessary roles that women play in supporting and running its everyday survival. Clearly, Boko Haram is willing to adapt to the culture and necessity of women in combative roles that it demands if the organization wants increased domestic and international attention and legitimacy.

Boko Haram has developed into a modernized realm of warfare that shares characteristics and has developed in the like of well-established and internationally renowned organizations. As a result, when the international community and Nigeria in particular work to plan against and combat them, they must take into consideration and adjust to the uniqueness of the organization's incorporation of women in particular and underlying issues that Boko Haram embodies in order to combat and eradicate them as a threat within the region. To date, the government of Nigeria has not addressed the underlying and well-known grievances that have fueled Boko Haram as well as utilized its most valuable resource—women—and thus has not taken the necessary first step in working towards peace for its population from this organization.

1. Nigerian Response

In the counterinsurgency realm, the Center for Naval Analyses (CNA) generated eight best practices that, according to McQuaid and Asfura-Heim, should be considered in order for a government to be successful in combatting its respective terrorism threats.[192] McQuaid and Asfura-Heim argue that due to Boko Haram being an insurgency "sustained by localized grievances and conflict dynamics,"[193] the starting point for deriving an effective response is through counterinsurgency (COIN) tactics. McQuaid and Asfura-Heim outline these eight tactics as follows:

1. Devise a strategy that is built on an analytically derived conflict assessment

2. Implement a coordinated whole-of-government approach

3. Bolster government legitimacy

---

[192] McQuaid and Asfura-Heim, "Rethinking the U.S. Approach to Boko Haram: The Case for a Regional Strategy," 12.

[193] McQuaid and Asfura-Heim, "Rethinking the U.S. Approach to Boko Haram: The Case for a Regional Strategy."

4. Protect the population

5. Address the root causes of the conflict

6. Attack the insurgent network

7. Cut off support and eliminate sanctuaries

8. Pursue opportunities to reach a settlement to the conflict[194]

The Nigerian government has claimed to be taking a "soft-approach strategy" in building up its institutions in order to combat Boko Haram, while in reality has taken a heavy-handed counterterrorism approach that fails to address realities and root causes.[195] This approach is seemingly unsuccessful as McQuaid and Asfura-Heim explain that

> The conflict is also being perpetuated by the Nigerian government itself...[whose] approach has further alienated the already disaffected northeastern communities, which, for the most part, remain hesitant to cooperate with the security forces or provide them with the necessary intelligence required to pin-point, network-centric operations. Because the government is unable to conduct surgical strikes against the insurgents, its operations often result in indiscriminate killings—which expand the pool of potential insurgent recruits and solidify a sense that the government is an equally liable party to the violence. Moreover, despite an increased military presence in the north, the government has been unable to protect the population from Boko Haram attacks and retaliatory raids, and, as a result, has lost a great deal of credibility.[196]

This heavy-handed counterterrorism approach has instilled distrust among the population, failed to deter Boko Haram attacks, and ignored the root grievances of the Nigerian people, thus making it unsuccessful to date.

The Nigerian government has primarily worked to downplay the threat and negate the grievances of not only Boko Haram, but the population as a whole and has labelled its "soft-approach strategy" as the combative method of choice in order to appease the public and convince them that measures are being taken to work against Boko Haram.

---

[194] McQuaid and Asfura-Heim, 12.

[195] McQuaid and Asfura-Heim, 9.

[196] McQuaid and Asfura-Heim, 9.

This approach inevitably cannot work as a standalone solution in the fight to combat Boko Haram as it does not address the grievances of the organization and the people of Nigeria. There are many pathways to success in counterterrorism, but one that provides a comprehensive approach that addresses political, economic, and social grievances will be needed to defeat this threat.[197] Former President of Nigeria Goodluck Jonathan has on multiple occasions made claim that Nigeria's conflict with Boko Haram requires international assistance and in May 2013 declared a state of emergency in the northern states of Yobe, Borno, and Adamawa as the soft-approach method was not proving to be making much progress.[198] "In April 2014, President Jonathan's national security advisor, Sambo Dasuki, published a strategy aimed at winning over the population of the north. Its implementation would command significant Nigerian government resources…however, even were it to do so, the Dasuki strategy addresses fundamental, long-term challenges such as inadequate education; it is not a short-term fix for Boko Haram."[199] With the successful election and transfer of power to current President Muhammadu Buhari in 2015, the hope that strides will be made to encompass the eight best practices of counterterrorism, yet significant progress has yet to be seen with this administration.

The CNA Analysis & Solutions Corporation created a comprehensive report in 2015 that strategically laid out—in the context of each of the eight best practices—the steps that the Nigerian government would need to take in order to successfully be working towards eradication of the Boko Haram threat. In summation, the following steps must be met:

- Boko Haram must be recognized and treated not as merely a group of troublemakers that can be crushed by military or pacified with money but a legitimate organization whose grievances must be addressed.[200]

---

[197] Asfura-Heim and McQuaid, "Diagnosing the Boko Haram Conflict: Grievances, Motivations, and Institutional Resilience in Northeast Nigeria," vi.

[198] John Campbell, "U.S. Policy to Counter Nigeria's Boko Haram," *Council Special Report* (Council on Foreign Relations: Center for Preventive Action, November 2014), 9–13, www.cfr.org.

[199] Campbell, 14.

[200] McQuaid and Asfura-Heim, "Rethinking the U.S. Approach to Boko Haram: The Case for a Regional Strategy," 37.

- An overreliance of military forces will not solve the problem and cross-governmental agencies must be built up and integrated into the fight. Only with this whole-of-government approach will the agencies needed to counter this threat not only grow stronger but have the resources needed to effectively counter Boko Haram.[201]

- It is well established that the Nigerian government is ripe with corruption. Reduction of corruption is imperative and success will not be achievable unless addressed. Efforts should be targeted at the "complicit local political elites, religious leaders, military commanders, and law enforcement officers."[202] The public must see that this corruption is being combatted. By well broadcasting the accountability that these officials are being held to, not only will it begin to establish trust with the population again, but it will deter future corruption of other officials.[203]

- As stated multiple times previously in this chapter, the socio-economic grievances of the organization must be addressed. The disparities between the northern and southern regions must recognized by government and political reform must occur in order to bolster legitimacy among the population.[204]

- Militarily, a restructure should be considered from a counterterrorism approach in order to not only protect the population from future Boko Haram attacks but to train on posture and positioning, increased border security, and community relations. Emphasis should be focused towards

---

[201] McQuaid and Asfura-Heim, 37.

[202] McQuaid and Asfura-Heim, 37.

[203] McQuaid and Asfura-Heim, 37–38.

[204] McQuaid and Asfura-Heim, 37–38.

the funding, communications, recruitment, and movements of Boko Haram.[205]

- Lastly, continued push to negotiate a settlement with the organization in order to mitigate violence whilst changes are being made within government.[206]

- If the Nigerian government is serious about combatting and eradicating Boko Haram as a threat within both the region and internationally, these steps at a minimum must be addressed. The CNA's eight steps will not be enough though to stop the blatant manipulation and utilization of women, both voluntary and involuntary to gain international and domestic attention and legitimacy. In order to eradicate and effectively combat Boko Haram, the Nigerian government must utilize one of both parties' greatest assets, their women. Though unlike Boko Haram, the Nigerian government must trend down the path of empowerment vice martyrdom. Through proper education, legitimacy of institutions, and equality in positions of power, women are able to empower other women and encourage them to create reform throughout Nigeria.

To the credit of former President Goodluck Jonathan, Boko Haram is an international threat and international assistance is warranted, yet this is a domestically grown threat and one that will not subside unless Nigeria makes major strides and implements legitimate political reform. This reform must be upheld long-term and must make all efforts to address the socio-economic grievances raised by this organization. The U.S. government, on the other hand, has historically, and are presently playing a supporting role in the context of its relationship with Nigeria. This manifests in the fight against Boko Haram in a broad and ever evolving way. The overarching theme of this governmental relationship though is that the United States will protect and maintain its relationship with the Nigerian government above all else, as Nigeria has one of the fastest

---

[205] McQuaid and Asfura-Heim, 37–38.

[206] McQuaid and Asfura-Heim, 38.

growing economies in the world and is considered an anchor state within the African countries.

With his meeting in with United States in May 2018 with President Donald Trump, President Buhari was the first sub-Saharan African leader to visit the Oval Office during the Trump administration. This significant meeting was held in order to discuss the counterterrorism efforts that Nigeria would take in the coming years against Boko Haram. Within the past United States Presidential administrations, in order to support the Nigerian government the United States has taken a whole-of-government approach and has pursued an approach that focuses on democracy, military support, law enforcement, intelligence, development, and humanitarianism. Through promotion of this "whole-of-government approach," as well as providing training and equipment to government officials and law enforcement, and investing in programs to build up Nigerian infrastructure, the United States has tried to support the Nigerian government and enable self-help in order to combat this threat. Issues with this approach arise in the corruption and unwillingness to implement a "hard-approach strategy" by the Nigerian government.[207]

2. U.S. Response

As Boko Haram is currently posing an expanding threat to the three Nigerian neighbors that make up the Lake Chad region (Chad, Cameroon, and Niger), and the fact that the United States is allies with all three countries, it is imperative that the U.S. government support the eradication of this FTO. Moving forward in the fight to combat the Boko Haram threat within Nigeria and the surrounding Lake Chad region, the United States should strongly consider a few options, ones that enhance the legitimacy of socio-economic institutions and promote equality across both economic and gender lines. In order for the United States to take a stronger, more active approach to combating the Boko Haram threat, it could essentially take one of two major paths, the same supporting role but with more pressure on the Nigerian government, or a containment and combative

---

[207] McQuaid and Asfura-Heim, 13–38.

approach.[208] By committing to continue in a supporting role, the United States government must change policy in order to put more pressure on the Nigerian government to modify its strategy. This can be done by publicly denouncing the Nigerian government and openly stating failure to act against Boko Haram.[209] The risk with this plan though as the United States government wishes to maintain good relations with the government and this public shaming tactic would tarnish those relations and potentially push the Nigerian government into a defensive position where they must maintain public image and the motivation would not be met meet the intended goal. This would also pose to be a counterproductive course of action for the United States in terms of minimizing the manipulation of women within the Boko Haram organization. By internationally denouncing the Nigerian government and opening the door for strained relations, the U.S. government would lose any credibility and chance of influencing the growth of political, social, and economic institutions.

The U.S. government could also impose sanctions on exports and against Nigerian government officials who have been known to profit from this conflict and who are not actively working towards a comprehensive solution to the threat. As well, a position that since Boko Haram is an international threat, business is not to be conducted with Nigerian companies and officials as it poses a threat to national security.[210] This approach is strong, a hard line, very confrontational, and poses a great risk to the relations between nations. With Nigeria being an anchor state within Africa and one of the United States most important relationships within the region, it is vital that care and finesse be taken when formulating a plan. This course of action increases the risk of abducted women being used as pawns by Boko Haram. With historical patterns under consideration, the likelihood that Boko Haram will retaliate when hard lines are drawn against those that support their efforts is high. Retaliation with this organization has historically been the kidnapping of women for ransom or integration into the

---

[208] McQuaid and Asfura-Heim, 39–48.

[209] McQuaid and Asfura-Heim, 39.

[210] McQuaid and Asfura-Heim, 41.

organization, which is counterproductive to the end goal of minimizing female utilization.

Lastly, the final avenue for the United States to take in order to maintain a non-combative role with the threat of Boko Haram is the manipulation of foreign aid could be used as a pawn to pressure the Nigerian government to comply with a whole-of-government approach. The risk to this approach is that by penalizing the government, you are penalizing the population as a whole. In a country so riddled with economic inequality and poverty, by taking away foreign aid going towards critical institutions the United States government not only undermines the long-term development goals that it is working to achieve, but it undermines its reputation within institutions that don't play a role in countering the threat against Boko Haram.

The other option for the United States is to adopt a containment and combative approach, as the Nigerian government has not been executing adequate counterinsurgency measures to quell the threat.[211] It is not unfeasible that a containment approach be addressed and implemented by the United States to prevent the spread of Boko Haram outside of Nigeria. This approach would quell Boko Haram in the interim from taking control of Nigeria's neighboring countries, which would pose a significant security threat to Africa as a whole while maintaining a long-term goal of addressing the underlying issues that the organization demands Nigeria address. "If Boko Haram's momentum is not reversed, it could have serious consequences for the future of the region, and ultimately one day potentially pose a direct threat to the United States and its interests. A regional containment approach can thus be seen as preventative, with the aim of avoiding a scenario in which Boko Haram directly targets the United States."[212] Though the approach may leave addressing the source of Boko Haram until later date, maintaining control in surrounding countries would have significant strategic appeal in the long run. Without addressing the root grievances of the organization, this course of action fails to facilitate the desperately needed strong, fair, and legitimate institutions that

---

[211] McQuaid and Asfura-Heim, 45.

[212] McQuaid and Asfura-Heim, 47.

will facilitate equal opportunities for both men and women within government. These institutions are desperately needed in order to make strides in empowering women to be more active in their government vice opposing it.

B. CONCLUSION

Not only has Boko Haram adapted to a higher female representation within the combative ranks, but it was founded upon and gained domestic legitimacy based on Yusuf's preaching's of female inequality within Nigeria and the need for increased education. Women have been integrated into the building blocks of Boko Haram since its formation, but only when it reformed in 2009 did they become engrained in the combative side. Moving forward in the international fight against Boko Haram, tactics such as those outlined by the CNA must be analyzed and adapted in order to plan a unique attack against Boko Haram. Underlying issues must be addressed, the threat must be contained to the Nigerian borders, and the international community must put an end to the fetishization and global outcry of women in combat so as not to feed into their utilization within terrorist organizations. It is only through legitimate restructuring of the Nigerian government in order to minimize corruption and address the major underlying grievances through strong institutions that empower Nigerian women with equality and education Boko Haram has a chance of being quelled. Until that day, one person's terrorist will continue to be another person's freedom fighter, and the organization will grow in strength, numbers, and legitimacy. Meanwhile, women's involvement, both voluntary and involuntary will become increasingly prevalent, and the presence and legitimacy of Boko Haram among the international community will continue to grow.

LIST OF REFERENCES

Amnesty International, "Nigeria: Abducted Women and Girls Forced to Join Boko Haram Attacks." April 14, 2015. https://www.amnesty.org/en/latest/news/2015/04/nigeria-abducted-women-and-girls-forced-to-join-boko-haram-attacks/.

Asfura-Heim, Patricio, and Julia McQuaid. "Diagnosing the Boko Haram Conflict: Grievances, Motivations, and Institutional Resilience in Northeast Nigeria." *CNA Analysis & Solutions*, January 2015, 1–74.

BBC News, "Who Are the Taliban?" May 26, 2016. http://www.bbc.com/news/world-south-asia-11451718.

Bloom, Mia. *Bombshell: Women and Terrorism*. Philadelphia, PA: University of Pennsylvania Press, 2011.

Burke, Jason. "Al Qaeda." *Foreign Policy,* 142 (June 2004): 18–26.

Campbell, John. "U.S. Policy to Counter Nigeria's Boko Haram." *Council Special Report* (Council on Foreign Relations: Center for Preventive Action, November 2014), November 2014. www.cfr.org.

Cohn, Carol, ed. *Women & Wars*. Cambridge, UK: Polity Press, 2013.

Cragin, R. Kim, and Sara A. Daly.d *Women as Terrorists: Mothers, Recruiters, and Martyrs*. First. Santa Barbara, CA: ABC-CLIO, LLC, 2009.

Cunningham, Karla J. "Cross-Regional Trends in Female Terrorism." *Studies in Conflict & Terrorism* 26, no. 3 (2003): 171–95. https://doi.org/10.1080/10576100390211419.

Department of Homeland Security. Immigration and Nationality Act: Section 219, 8 USC § 1189 (2001). https://www.uscis.gov/ilink/docView/SLB/HTML/SLB/0-0-0-1/0-0-0-29/0-0-0-5017.html#0-0-0-220.

Franks, Mary Anne. "Obscene Undersides: Women and Evil Between the Taliban and the United States." *Hypatia,* 18, no. 1 (Winter 2003): 135–56.

Gaffey, Conor. "ISIS Just Started Using Female Suicide Bombers, but Boko Haram Has Been Doing It For Years - and Shows No Signs Of Stopping." *Newsweek*. August 12, 2017. http://www.newsweek.com/isis-boko-haram-nigeria-suicide-bomber-649790.

Gunaratna, Rohan, and Aviv Oreg. "Al Qaeda's Organizational Structure and Its Evolution." *Studies in Conflict & Terrorism* 33, no. 12 (November 20, 2010): 1043–78. https://doi.org/10.1080/1057610X.2010.523860.

Gunaratna, Rohan. *Inside Al Qaeda: Global Network of Terror*. New York.: Cambridge University Press, 2002.

Hearne, Ellie B. "Participants, Enablers, and Preventers: The Roles of Women in Terrorism." In *British International Studies Association Annual Conference*, 1–15. Leicester, UK, 2009. https://is.muni.cz/el/1423/jaro2010/MVZ203/Gender___Terrorism__BISA__Hearne__Dec_2009.pdf.

International Crisis Group. *Nigeria: Women and the Boko Haram Insurgency*. Brussels, Belgium: International Crisis Group, 2016. https://www.crisisgroup.org/africa/west-africa/nigeria/nigeria-women-and-boko-haram-insurgency.

Jenkins, Brian Michael. "The Study of Terrorism: Definitional Problems." Santa Monica, CA: RAND, December 1980. http://www.dtic.mil/docs/citations/ADA103363.

Johnson, Thomas H. *Taliban Narratives: The Use and Power of Stories in the Afghanistan Conflict*. New York, N.Y.: Oxford University Press, 2017.

Johnson, Thomas H. "Taliban Adaptations and Innovations." *Small Wars & Insurgencies* 24, no. 1 (2013): 3–27. https://doi.org/10.1080/09592318.2013.740228.

Johnson, Thomas H. "The Taliban Insurgency and an Analysis of Shabnamah (Night Letters)." *Small Wars & Insurgencies* 18, no. 3 (September 2007): 317–44. https://doi.org/10.1080/09592310701674176.

Kepel, Gilles. *Jihad: The Trail of Political Islam*. Trans. Anthony Roberts. Cambridge, MA: The Belknap Press of Harvard University Press, 2002.

Kramer, Mark. "Guerrilla Warfare, Counterinsurgency and Terrorism in Teh North Caucasus: The Military Dimension of the Russian - Chechen Conflict." *Europe-Asia Studies* 57, no. 2 (2005): 209–90. https://doi.org/10.1080/09668130500051833.

Kurz, Robert W., and Charles K. Bartles. "Chechen Suicide Bombers." *The Journal of Slavic Military Studies* 20, no. 4 (2007): 529–47. https://doi.org/10.1080/13518040701703070.

Leede, Seran de. "Afghan Women and the Taliban: An Exploratory Assessment." In *ICCT Policy Brief*, 1–13. Hague, Netherlands: International Centre for Counter-Terrorism - The Hague, 2014. www.icct.nl.

Lindemann, Katherine. "Female Terrorists - A Surprisingly Timeless Phenomenon." *Researchgate* (blog), December 21, 2015. https://www.researchgate.net/blog/post/female-terrorists-a-surprisingly-timeless-phenomenon.

Lower, Wendy. *Hitler's Furies: German Women in the Nazi Killing Fields*. Reprint. Wilmington, MA: Mariner Books, 2014.

Matfess, Hilary. *Women and the War on Boko Haram: Wives, Weapons, Witnesses.*
London, England: Zed Books, 2017. http://www.zedbooks.net.

McQuaid, Julia, and Patricio Asfura-Heim. "Rethinking the U.S. Approach to Boko
Haram: The Case for a Regional Strategy." *CNA Analysis & Solutions*, February
2015. https://www.cna.org/cna_files/pdf/DRM-2014-U-009462-Final.pdf.

Ness, Cindy D. *Female Terrorism and Militancy: Agency, Utility, and Organization.*
New York, N.Y.: Routledge, 2008.

Pape, Robert A. *Dying to Win: The Strategic Logic of Suicide Terrorism.* New York:
Random House, 2006.

Roessler, Philip. *Ethnic Politics and State Power in Africa: The Logic of the Coup-Civil
War Trap.* Cambridge, UK: Cambridge University Press, 2016.

Sciolino, Elaine, and Souad Mekhennet. "Al-Qaeda Warrior Uses Internet to Rally
Women." *New York Times.* May 28, 2008.

Skinner, Ania. "The Rising Trend of Female Suicide Bombers in Nigeria." *The Fund for
Peace - Global Square* (blog), March 28, 2015. http://library.fundforpeace.org/
blog-20150328-nigeriawomenbombers.

Speckhard, Anne. "Female Terrorists in ISIS, Al Qaeda and 21rst Century Terrorism."
Trends Research: Inside the Mind of a Jihadist, May 2015.
http://trendsinstitution.org/wp-content/uploads/2015/05/Female-Terrorists-in-
ISIS-al-Qaeda-and-21rst-Century-Terrorism-Dr.-Anne-Speckhard.pdf.

Speckhard, Anne, and Khapta Akhmedova. *Black Widows: The Chechen Female Suicide
Terrorists.* Tel Aviv: Jaffee Center for Strategic Studies: Tel Aviv University,
2006. http://www.inss.org.il/publication/black-widows-chechen-female-suicide-
terrorists/?offset=0&posts=1&type=405&outher=Anne%20Speckhard.

Speckhard, Anne, and Khapta Akhmedova. "The Making of a Martyr: Chechen Suicide
Terrorism." *Studies in Conflict & Terrorism* 29, no. 5 (September 22, 2006): 429–
92. https://doi.org/10.1080/10576100600698550.

Stanford University, CISAC, "Mapping Militant Organizations: Boko Haram." August
26, 2016. http://web.stanford.edu/group/mappingmilitants/cgi-bin/groups/view/
553?highlight=boko+haram.

Thurston, Alexander. *Boko Haram: The History of an African Jihadist Movement.*
Princeton, NJ: Princeton University Press, 2018.

U.S. Army War College Press, and Strategic Studies Institute. *Female Suicide Bombers.*
CreateSpace Independent Publishing Platform, 2015.

U.S. Department of State. "Foreign Terrorist Organizations." Accessed August 6, 2017. https://www.state.gov/j/ct/rls/other/des/123085.htm.

Von Knop, Katharina. "The Female Jihad: Al Qaeda's Women." *Studies in Conflict & Terrorism* 30, no. 5 (2007): 397–414. https://doi.org/10.1080/10576100701258585.

Waal, Thomas de. "Analysis: Chechnya's Endless War." BBC News, April 23, 2001. http://news.bbc.co.uk/2/hi/europe/1292799.stm.

Zedalis, Debra D. "Female Suicide Bombers" (U.S. Army War College: Strategic Studies Institute, 2004), https://ssi.armywarcollege.edu/pdffiles/pub408.pdf

Zenn, Jacob, and Elizabeth Pearson. "Women, Gender and the Evolving Tactics of Boko Haram." *Journal of Terrorism Research* 5, no. 1 (February 2014): 46–57. https://doi.org/10.15664.

INITIAL DISTRIBUTION LIST

1.	Defense Technical Information Center
	Ft. Belvoir, Virginia

2.	Dudley Knox Library
	Naval Postgraduate School
	Monterey, California

Printed in Great Britain
by Amazon